HEREWA

The Siege of the Isle of Ely and Involvement of
Together with

DE GESTIS HERWARDI SAXONIS
(The Exploits of Hereward the Saxon)

Researched and compiled in the 12th century by Monastery Historians
Revised and re-written in modern English by TREVOR A. BEVIS. 1981

The publisher acknowledges the kindness of the Very Rev. Randolph Wise, Dean of Peterborough, Canon Christie, Chancellor and Librarian of Peterborough Cathedral in allowing him to publish the Gestis Herwardi. His gratitude also to Peterborough Museum Society for permission to extract paragraphs from The Peterborough Chronicle of Hugh Candidus, and the Dean and Chapter of Ely Cathedral for permission to quote matter from the Liber Eliensis. The publisher records his appreciation to Sir Hereward Wake, Bart., M.C., D.L., for his interest and help, and to all who assisted in any way.

WESTRYDALE PRESS
T. Bevis, 28 St Peters Road, March, Cambs PE15 9NA

COPYRIGHT © 1982 — T. A. Bevis

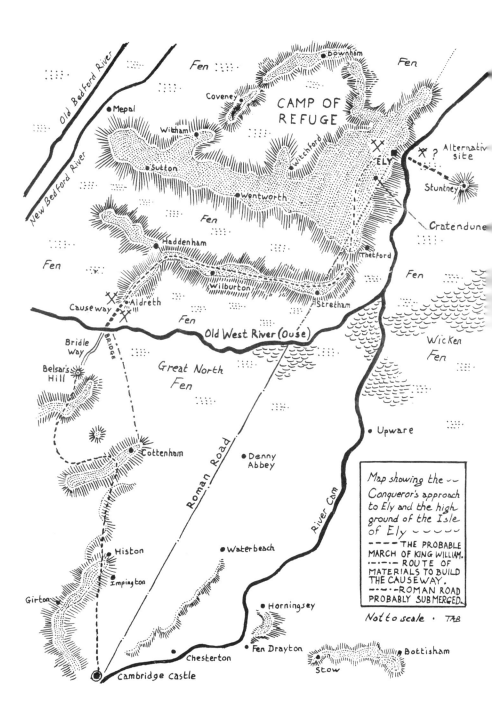

Map showing the
Conqueror's approach
to Ely and the high
ground of the Isle
of Ely

---- THE PROBABLE
MARCH OF KING WILLIAM.
·-·-·- ROUTE OF
MATERIALS TO BUILD
THE CAUSEWAY.
-~·- ROMAN ROAD
PROBABLY SUBMERGED.

Not to scale · TAB

Preface

By SIR HEREWARD WAKE, Bart., M.C., D.L.

Much has been written about the Saxon patriot, Hereward. Eminent writers have produced novels to fire the imagination, but mixing fact with fiction tends to relegate heroes to the realm of myth. The purpose of this book is to prove that Hereward did exist and that the Isle of Ely formed the backcloth to his inspiring achievements against a more numerical and formidable foe.

History bequeaths sufficient evidence written by Church scholars of the authenticity of this remarkable siege — the final attempt by the Saxon hierarchy to usurp the invader and regain liberty. Accounts from the monastic manuscript "De Gestis Herwardi Saxonis" outline events in the epic siege and relate a great deal more about that outstanding Englishman, Hereward, and his adventures abroad. It is a wonderful thing to read this account from the pen of a reputable monk-historian who, aware of the incredulity of readers, stated that his research for most part was based on the knowledge of men then living, namely Hereward's colleagues-at-arms. We can arrive no nearer the truth than that.

Hereward Wake

Courteenhall, Northampton.

Introduction

"De Gestis Herwardi Saxonis" is undoubtedly the oldest existing manuscript touching upon the exploits of Hereward, a Saxon patriot of the 11th Century, the fame of whom is traditionally known in places where English is spoken. The transcript gives expanded contractions from the Latin, in places corrupt and the grammar inaccurate, the fault of the scribe. In this publication proper names are spelt with a capital unlike those in the manuscript, and modern phrases used, care being taken to preserve the meaning of the original work.

In the past some said that the monks' work was ficticious and Hereward a figment of the imagination. Why, then, should the authors - possessors of knowledge and of considerable intellect - devote such obvious care and much time on work painstakingly researched, were there no truth in it? The man that wrote it and his assistants believed in the Fatherhood of God and the brotherhood of man. Being so dedicated and ruled by conscience they surely placed strong emphasis on truth. Hereward is traditionally known as The Wake, this believed by some to have been added after his lifetime through a descendant marrying into the Wake family. Genealogists have shown a long line of descent in this family and a number of confirmative articles have appeared on the subject. (See end paper).

The "Gestis Herwardi" was edited by T.D. Hardy and C.T. Martin in "Lestorie des Engles solum la translacion Maistre Geffrei Gaimer", Rolls Series 1883, vol. I pp. 339-404. The latin text was printed with an English translation as an addendum to Fenland Notes and Queries, vol. III 1895-1897 (Rev. W.D. Sweeting, M.A.). Transcription had been undertaken earlier by S.H. Miller, F.R.A.M.S. It was revised and re-written by the present writer in 1981 and for the first time appears in this edition.

Delving into the past is fascinating but fraught with pitfalls and it must be considered that the monks' work may include hearsay. Nevertheless it should be borne in mind that there were witnesses and their contributions with that of literary fragments by Leofric the Deacon must place greater degrees of truth on the matter than does doubt. In this publication the "Gestis Herwardi" is preceded by researched work from the previous editions in which I endeavoured to justify the monastery historians' literary prowess of almost nine centuries ago and give some authenticity to the epic siege of that most historic bastion, the Isle of Ely, and the involvement of the monasteries of Ely and Peterborough rich in Hereward tradition - their sites now graced with exquisite Norman cathedrals.

Trevor Bevis

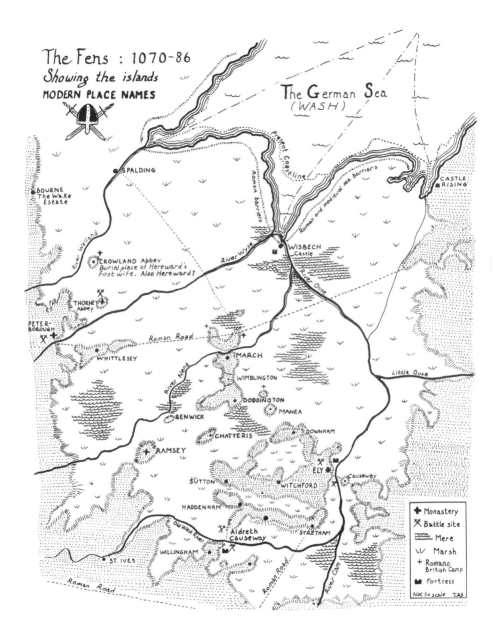

The Fens : 1070-86
Showing the islands
MODERN PLACE NAMES

The German Sea
(WASH)

Present Coastline

Roman barriers

Roman and medieval sea barriers

SPALDING

BOURNE
The Wake
Estate

River Welland

River Wyse

CROWLAND Abbey
Burial place of Hereward's
First wife. Also Hereward?

WISBECH
Castle

River Ouse

CASTLE
RISING

THORNEY
Abbey

PETER-
BOROUGH

Roman Road

WHITTLESEY

River Nene

MARCH

WIMBLINGTON

DODDINGTON

MANEA

Little Ouse

BENWICK

CHATTERIS

DOWNHAM

RAMSEY

SUTTON

ELY

WITCHFORD

Causeway

HADDENHAM

Old West River

Aldreth
Causeway

STRETHAM

WILLINGHAM

ST. IVES

Roman Road

Roman Road

River Cam

✚	Monastery
✕	Battle site
〰	Mere
\⅃/	Marsh
+	Romano British Camp
⌂	Fortress

Not to scale   TAB

The Historic Fens

Portrayed against the historically rich background of the Isle of Ely, this account of Hereward The Wake and his defence of the Isle is broadly based upon the knowledge and research of monastic scholars of credible reputation. Famous for its dramatic links with the past the Isle had been fortified by Saxons and Danes long before Hereward's time. The first Danish attack upon the Isle was repulsed but on the second onslaught in the 9th Century the sea rovers overcame obstinate resistance and the Saxon defenders were put to flight. Many nobles who had enjoyed sanctuary in the Fens, were killed. The Danes sailed their longboats along the Ouse and into the labyrinth of rivers and meres. One was actually discovered in a field near Manea in the 1800's. Within a year most of it had been chopped to pieces for kindling! The Danes inhabited the Isle until they were driven out during the reign of Edward. Years later they returned despoiling the monasteries at Ely, Peterborough, Ramsey, Thorney and Crowland. Not surprisingly the Fen people were a mixed race, principally Saxon incorporating Scandinavian blood. Some Danes settled down to farm and became Christians, adopting the style of the Gyrwas (men of the marsh). The Fenmen were a hardy, long suffering race, fierce when occasion necessitated it and very independent, a characteristic which prevails to this day. Between 1066 and 1071 more armed Danes entered the Isle.

Matthew Paris, in his "Chronica Majora" compiled in the 13th Century, made many references to the Fens, including the following statement : "AD 1071. The Earls Edwin, Morcar and Siward with Egelwin, Bishop of Durham, associated themselves with many thousand disaffected persons and rebels against William the First. At first they betake themselves to the forest and waste plains; then they do what mischief they can to the King's property in various places, and finally seek a place of refuge in the Isle of Ely. There, under the leadership of Hereward the Wake, they make frequent sallies and do much damage....The King, coming against them, surrounds the Isle with his forces, makes roads and bridges, renders the deep swamps passable for man and beast and builds the castle at Wisbech".

Edwin was slain at the very beginning of the rebellion. Morcar and Siward were taken prisoners when the Isle of Ely lay under siege, but their lives were spared. They were among those whom the King on his death bed, ordered to be set free. Egelwin the Bishop was also taken prisoner and sent to Abington where he soon died.

Several years elapsed before England was totally conquered. While William The Conqueror was engaged in putting down rebellions in the north, insurrections were rife in the south. Most of the rebellions were suppressed by the King's lieutenants but the problem in the West required the Conqueror's personal prowess to bring the insurgents to submission. The Northumbrian uprising was repeated on the banks of the Dee and the Mersey, these put down with savage ferocity. The most renowned of the uprisings took place in the Fens, where were gathered Saxons, Danes and "men from Berkshire...and everything bade fair for a long defence." The ensuing struggle was probably the King's most worrying time. Protected by treacherous marsh the islanders were short of nothing and here the Church was strong. The Fenland was regarded as the holy land of the English for it contained famous religious establishments: Ely, Peterborough, Ramsey, Crowland, Thorney with their succursal cells and several smaller monasteries. The area was ideal for defensive strategy and it is fair to say that the King did not suppress it through military strength. The end was brought about through submission by the Church, called by many an act of treachery.

The Normans probed the Isle of Ely from different points, sometimes from the direction of Soham and from near Reach, weapons having been discovered between these places and the Isle. Details of attacks are meagre but it is evident that the Normans were repulsed on the waterways and that the island garrison took up the role of commandos, devising hit and run tactics. The Normans attempted to build a causeway across a narrow strip of fen between Aldreth and the Old West River. There, apparently, took place the greatest of Hereward's English exploits. His organised attacks on the Conqueror's workforce and soldiers were said to be "sudden, mysterious and murderous". Abbot Thurstan and his monks are credited as giving the King the cue which led to the reduction of the Isle. The Abbot went to Warwick to make his submission. He had to make the most abject obedience to assuage the King's wrath.

1

In the "Liber Eliensis" (Ely Book), compiled in the 12th Century, it is written that the monks to their sorrow met the displeased King at Witchford. "Afterwards as the King was leaving (Ely monastery) Gilbert de Clare came in to see the monastery and after looking everywhere, found the monks at dinner in the refectory. 'Oh, wretched and foolish men,' he said, 'to sit here stuffing yourselves at this of all times, when the King is here and in your church', and thereupon they forsook the tables and rushed to the church but could not find the King. Much perturbed and having little hope save in God's providence they besought Gilbert to intercede for them with the King lest ill befall. This he agreed to do and was able with some difficulty to obtain for them an audience with the view to averting the royal wrath by prayers or presents. And being brought before the King at Witchford where he then was, through the mediation of Gilbert and other nobles they were received back into favour at the price of 700 marks of silver."

When at last the struggle had ended, William held a Council of Enquiry at Kentford, Suffolk, the issue being "the Church of Ely was put in possession of all the Rights, Customs and Privileges it enjoyed at the time of King Edward's death" (Bentham). The Conqueror fixed for Ely monastery 40 knights' fees and refused to take a money consideration in lieu thereof. This was the number of Norman soldiers the abbey had to maintain, and it was intended as a humilatory condition. Worse was to come. William Rufus, the King' son, demanded double this number to help him suppress the insurrection which favoured Robert.

Peterborough monk, Hugh Candidus, esteemed historian and compiler of the Peterborough Chronicle - an early 12th Century manuscript - evocably outlines the early life of the Church at Medehamstede (Peterborough). He and his assistants have been attributed with the work alluding to the life of Hereward, although this is by no means certain. Over the centuries several historians commented upon the siege of the Isle of Ely and Hereward's role in its defence. His father's estate was seized by the Normans and Hereward who had spent a great deal of time abroad applying his skill in military matters was prompted into action by personal vendetta and patriotism. He accepted the invitation to lead the struggle against the despised invader. The choice of battle ground was admirable from the Saxons' point of view, the Isle of Ely then an island sanctuary surrounded by impassable marsh. It was an ideal base from which to conduct organised resistance. The "leader of the soldiers" was severely criticised for his planned assault upon Peterborough monastery, especially as he had employed a force of Danes to carry it out.

Monastery Plundered

The final years of wearisome and sanguinary incursions by the Danish hordes culminated in an astonishing alliance between Saxons and their fierce adversaries. On 14th October, 1066, the result of the Battle of Hastings introduced the end of the Saxon epoch and forced a distrustful peace between the races. The Danes - no strangers to the Fens - played no small part in Hereward's plan to disrupt and harrass William The Conquerer's army. Skirmishes took place around the Isle of Ely, the insurgents emerging from their fastness to engage the Normans in lightning assaults. Not surprisingly Hugh Candidus was not slow to write his abhorence of Hereward's attitude to the Church and its possessions. Hereward had no reservations at striking out at such authority when it suited him. He did this at Peterborough on two occasions and was quite ready to set fire to Ely monastery after the monks had betrayed him. On the demise of Hereward's uncle, Abbot Brando, the King appointed a Frenchman, Turold (as was his policy) to Peterborough monastery with its excessively rich possessions. Hereward was aware of Turold's stern reputation and granted him scant respect. An intense hatred of each other sprang up between the two men. Turold stayed at Stamford prior to his appointment and had with him several Knights. The new Abbot was not liked and he had a strong military leaning. Gunton wrote: "He being a stranger neither loved his monastery, nor his convent him". It is thought that the monks (being good Saxons) occasionally rebelled against Turold and that he caused a castle to be built on a mound known as Tout Hill, north of the monastery, that he might enjoy greater authority over the brethren and town.

Hereward, concerned over the appointment, planned a "commando" raid upon the monastery before the new Abbot seized possession. He sent a force of Danes to take whatever there was in books, gold and silver, relics and other precious things. He did this, he said, to prevent the valuables from falling into Norman hands. This plan came to the monks' notice and one, Ivo the sacrist, advised by worried brethren of Hereward's design, collected together as many items as possible including gospel texts, chasubles and copes and hurried to Stamford where he disclosed the plan to Turold. Meanwhile Hereward's army embarked and made its way through the marshes and meres and along rivers, arriving at Peterborough on 2nd June, 1069. Hugh Candidus wrote that this force promptly attacked Bolhithe Gate, a fortified entrance to the monastery precincts believed to have stood on or near the site of the present Bishop's Road gardens, not far from the river Nene. According to the chronicler, writing 40-50 years later, a strenuous battle occurred but the monks, protected by high walls and buildings, held out. The raiders eventually set fire to the buildings and forced the gateway. They burnt everything except one house and the church.

Desperate to save the church the monks entreated the Danes to refrain from this great wrong, but unheeding their pleas the raiders entered the monastery, the foundations of which are still visible. Attracted to the great cross the men would have borne it away but were not able. Thereupon they seized the golden crown from the crucifix set with precious stones and also took the footrest fashioned from pure gold and encrusted with gems. They also took two golden feretories and carried the spoils to the waiting boats. The feretories contained relics including the holy arm of St. Oswald. Before departing, the raiders broke into the great tower where was hidden a huge table of gold and silver, aglow with precious and semi-precious gems. In times of peace the table occupied a place near the high altar. They seized in the same place nine feretories and 12 crosses. The chronicler wrote: "of all the treasures none as good as those remained in England." These previous items with a large number of valuable books had given prestige to Peterborough and by these same acquisitions the town had been renamed Gildenburgh (golden borough). Sadly, after this attack the town became one of the poorest in the land.

Hereward tolerated much criticism for his part in this destructive excursion. Hugh Candidus made this personal observation: "They (the raiders) said they did this out of loyalty to the church and the Danes would guard these things better than the Frenchmen for the use of the church. And indeed Hereward was himself a man of the monks and for that reason many believed in him." Many times in later years Hereward swore that his soldiers entered the monastery with good intentions. He declared that by seizing the monastery's valuables he had saved them for the Church and at the same time delivered a blow at the Normans. The resistance from the Isle of Ely was largely inspired by King William's insistence in replacing Saxon priests with French churchmen. The items conveyed by Ivo the sacrist to Abbot Turold were returned to Peterborough but most of the church possessions seized by Hereward were lost forever. Initially these were taken to Ely. The Danes took with them Prior Aethelwold and a monk called Egelsin and a few of his colleagues. The silver and gold was given to the Danes. At Gildenburgh consternation and despair descended upon the community. They that remained became scattered and divided and Abbot Turold found only one monk named Leofwin Lange who was ill in the infirmary. Thus was fulfilled Bishop Aethelric's prophecy that at an appointed hour the monks would be driven out and the church goods despoiled. Turold arrived with between 140 and 160 heavily armed Knights. His bitterness in not finding the despoilers became more acute when he beheld the scorched buildings and learned of the theft of the church treasure, which by then was well away on the waterways of the vast Fens.

The heavily laden boats arrived safely at the Camp of Refuge some 30 miles away, and Prior Aethelwold stepped ashore with weary heart. A well loved man was the Prior gifted with wisdom and he possessed not a little cunning. The Danes trusted and respected him; they even invited him to go with them to their own country and promised him that he would become their Bishop. The Prior pretended to accept their offer and as a further indication of their trust they placed him in charge of the ill-gotten treasure and let him have possession of the keys to the chests. One day (wrote Hugh Candidus) the Danes feasted merrily in the great hall. This provided Aethelwold with a suitable opportunity to explore the feretories. He posted two servants at strategic positions, one with the Danes, the other nearby. Taking tools he began to remove gold and silver, and eventually exposed a heavily banded wooden chest which the Prior opened with difficulty. Inside he discovered a receptacle containing the arm of St. Oswald with various other relics. Great fear descended upon him and he quickly hid the relics in straw which formed a pillow for his head. Later Aethelwold resilvered them to their original style and while doing so was almost discovered by the Danes, rising for Vespers. Sluggish with drink they were in no hurry to remove themselves and the Prior completed his labours then prepared himself for the service.

Next day Hereward ordered Aethelwold to go with the Danes to their country. Unwilling to do this the Prior called his servants and prepared them as though to convey goods to Peterborough. He told them, however, that the relics must be taken to Ramsey Abbey for safe keeping. Meanwhile King William was reconciled with the King of Denmark, and it was agreed that the Danes keep any treasure they had taken from England. At Ely, the Danes gathered together their loot and sailed away from the Fens. When out at sea a terrible storm broke upon the vessels and divided them, forcing some upon distant shores. But the great table from Peterborough monastery (then called Gildenburgh) arrived at its new destination together with a few feretories and a crucifix or two. These were taken to a Danish Church. Later, Ivor the sacrist of Gildenburgh obtained leave to go to Denmark and manged to repossess some of his monastery's treasures. These were put aboard a vessel and returned to Peterborough.

The Epic Siege

The monastery historian's account of the Dane's attack upon the abbey underlines the fear and uncertainty of the country when King William was hard put to establish his iron will upon the inhabitants. In the Fens the monarch, a man of fair justice generally, faced brave and resourceful adversaries and he soon discovered that the Saxon leaders and their army matched the military prowess of his generals and soldiers from Normandy. The insurgents wasted no time in fortifying the Isle of Ely, taking advantage of the environment - the marshes and meres. Communications between the islands was maintained via the river system and certain causeways could be used during summer months. There is some uncertainty as to how long the insurgents held the Isle; they had established themselves there before Hereward arrived on the scene. The defeats at York and Northumbria, and that in the west in particular did not dampen the spirits of the Saxon nobles and they decided to make one more attempt to overthrow the King from the security of the Isle. A scribe wrote that the Saxons resisted the King for seven years, this in all probability taking into account the years from Senlac Field (1066) to the time of the conflict at Ely and finally in Northamptonshire. Another chronicler penned that the rebellion at Ely continued for three years; yet another ascribed the view that the Ely struggle lasted 18 months and one would think that is nearer the truth.

King William conducted his campaigns ruthlessly. His reduction of York well illustrates his attitude to rebellion, but in all fairness only once did he order the execution of an eminent Saxon, namely Earl Waltheof who was later enshrined at Crowland. Although he acted promptly and efficiently wherever rebellion occurred he regarded his campaigns in other parts of the country as less serious than the uprising in the Fens. For that reason he recalled his army from the north and distributed it around the Fen perimeter. It cost the King dearly in lives. Hereward joined the Ely resistance by invitation and was appointed leader of the soldiers; he enjoyed the support of three powerful Saxon Earls. All the bravest and most faithful of English manhood rallied around the defiant standard flying proudly from the Isle of Ely. Earls, bishops, abbots, famous soldiers, indeed the wisest and noblest in the land assembled at the Camp of Refuge. Their courage was openly admired by the King and he confronted them with his best warriors.

The monarch had erected a motte and bailey castle at Cambridge the earthworks of which still remain. From there it was convenient for soldiers to reach the Midlands and the north, the Fens making approach in that direction impossible. The strategic castle at Cambridge was probably on the insurgents' minds as well. Their unassailable position on the Isle of Ely overlooked the southern Fen plain not far from which stretched the old Roman highway from Cambridge to Huntingdon. It was an ominous outlook and it represented a double threat to the King's security: (1) Molestment of commercial and military users of the highway; (2) foraging parties laying waste and setting fire to the countryside. With each passing week would come a strengthening boost for insurgents and with it the distinct possibility of the rebellion gaining such momentum as to break out of the Fens and involve other provinces. Goaded by the Conqueror's arbitrary measures the beleaguered Saxons and their Scandinavian allies secured the watery fastness for a prolonged seige. Matthew Paris 13th century historian, wrote that a wooden fortress stood on the Isle of Ely, known as "Hereward's Castle". Bentham (p.104) writing of the Normans' forward position, says "The camp that was occupied by the Conqueror's army when he besieged the Isle of Ely is still visible at the south end of Aldrey Causeway within the manor of Wiveingham (Willingham), and is corruptly called "Belsar's Hills".

Aldreth is a name changed through the centuries. "The main approach was not by the two great Roman roads, Akeman Street and Via Devana, but at a point called Aedreth, a corruption of the patron saint Aethelthryth (Etheldreda)". (Freeman, Norman Conquest, vol.IV, p.464). The same author on page 465, states : "In the Gestis Herwardi (57) the place "Abrehede...ubi minusiquis et palude proecingitur (insular)'. In the Ely History (Liber secundus) 229, it is: 'Alrehethe ubi aquae insula latae sunt.'

Why did not the King lead his army along Akeman Street directly from Cambridge castle to Ely? This road crossing the Old West River with two extensive meres in the vicinity for much of the year was probably submerged. According to historians William took the route north via Histon to Cotinglade (Cottenham). Materials (stones, trees, hides, etc.,) were transported there in preparation for the laying down of a causeway across the narrow strip of marsh towards the Isle of Ely.

Determined to crush resistance the King hastened to the area with "his whole army," stationing his soldiers at strategic points. He hoped to neutralise the resistance with all speed but reckoned without the insurgents' advantage in their choice of battleground. In 1066 the marshes of Senlac Field trapped numbers of Norman cavalrymen; as it happened a similar fate awaited large numbers of footsoldiers near the Isle of Ely. The King caused a stockade to be erected at Reach and it is thought another was built at Earith, eight miles from Reach overlooking the fateful corridor of marsh. Life upon the Isle of Ely could not have been bad. The defenders were entirely self-sufficient and we are told that Earls and Knights regularly dined in the refectory of Ely monastery. Furthermore, the monks themselves were well equipped and well versed in the art of warfare - "a marvellous thing" commented a captured Norman Knight, on seeing them. The Abbot of Ely, trusting in the financial and natural resources of his rich and powerful domain contemplated a victory of sorts. He sustained the fighting men and received the backing of the Saxon Primate of England. Much in Abbot Thurstan's mind was the inevitable fact that a long-drawn-out seige could only result in the insurgents' defeat and that the King would be unmerciful. In any case sooner or later he would have to surrender his church and its possessions to a Norman abbot. If the Saxons were to enjoy the sustained fruits of victory and usurp the King, it had to be done quickly.

An interesting account of the King's opening and disastrous assault upon the Isle is given in the Magna Britannia. When the stockade at Reach had been erected, William ordered a rendezvous of his army opposite the Isle "...where the fen was four furlongs in breadth. He caused a bridge or causeway to be made of wood, stone and faggots of all kinds with trees and great pieces of timber fastened underneath with cowhides; but this structure proved so insecure that the greater part of his army in attempting to pass it were drowned in the fens. He now gave over for the present any further attempts to subdue his enemies in the island and retired with the remains of his army, leaving certain guards of soldiers on the borders of the Fens to prevent them laying waste the neighbouring country. Some incursions nevertheless were made by the islanders in one of which they set fire to the town of Burwell and had a successful skirmish with some soldiers from the King's garrison at Reach." (A detailed account given in "De Gestis Herwardi"). It would appear that this alludes to Aldreth, the controversial causeway's traditional site.

Some have it that the more likely site lay between Stuntney and Ely, a distance of about two miles. Was it there that the King attempted to subjugate the Isle, or did he approach the land from the direction of Willingham some distance to the south? Did William in fact try from one direction and fail and then move his army to the second site (two attempts are recorded), only to fail again? The Stuntney theory has root in its logical military advantage, using Stuntney as a stepping stone to the Isle. "Alderforth" Farm nearby lends more weight; some believe it is a corruption of Aldreth. W. Dring, in his Fenland Story, wrote: "In 1924, workmen dredging the river near Braham Farm, a mile south of Ely, found several spearheads of Saxon and Norman type and some bones." It is unwise to place too much emphasis on the discovery of ancient weapons as it is a fact that the Fen islands were well populated in Saxon times. A leaf-shaped bronze sword was found on Aldreth Causeway many years ago and this may well imply that this causeway existed long before the Norman Conquest. There is one significant thing, at least. The writer personally examined a sackful of Saxon-Norman type weapons zealously guarded by a retired fen roder who had discovered them while cleaning out ditches between Upware and Reach.

From Roman times, at least, Aldreth Causeway provided access to the greensand ridge until such time when the Fens became inundated and the "Way" became partially impassable. The Causeway was a continuation of a bridleway to Willingham called the Mere or Mare Way. It was protected by a circular fortified camp, known as Belsar's Hill, probably a British earthwork. This entrenchment protected the free passage along the "Way". Stukeley refers to the earthwork as "a Roman camp repaired by the Conqueror's soldiers". The camp is believed to be named after Belasius, reputed to be the Norman general supervising operations during the siege. Little is know about him. A chronicler wrote that Belasius was a Roman soldier. Another penned that he "was famous among the rebels in the Conqueror's time when the King built Cambridge castle." Fuller refers to Belasius as "one of the Knights quartered in the monastery at Ely", a statement founded on the "Tabular Eliensis" which apparently commemorates the departure of the Norman Knights who had been placed at Ely after its surrender. It is significant that the name of Belasius is recorded in this.

The existence of Belsar's Hill and its apparent association with the siege of the Isle of Ely must have some credible bearing on Aldreth Causeway being the scene of the disastrous attempt to take the Isle. The writer of "De Gestis Herwardi" refers to a place called "Alrehede" near a "great river" (the Ouse). Alrehede could mean Aldreth - or an area in the vicinity of Alderforth Farm, near Stuntney. The problem is made more difficult in that the "great river" cuts the causeway at Stuntney in two; just past the greensand ridge near Stretham the river veers right and does exactly the same thing between Willingham and Aldreth! Probing into history as deep as this brings out the mists and it is a fact that no-one can be one hundred per cent certain - unless one has implicit trust in monastery historians' accounts on such matters.

Whichever direction the attacks were made makes little difference. The cessation of hostilities probably centred on Cratendune, a Saxon settlement approximately a mile south of Ely of which nothing remains, save a few items taken from the soil and displayed in Ely Museum. There is mention of "Hereward's Castle". Hereward is supposed to have had a dislike of fortifications, but there had to be a place where his soldiers where quartered, and it may well have been at Cratendune. According to "De Gestis Herwardi" Hereward with his most notable soldiers, forewarned of the Normans' entry into the Isle managed to escape. Others may well have made a final stand against the King who according to the chronicler crowned his shallow victory with a visit to Ely monastery.

It seems incredible that the King attempted a second time to subjugate the Isle by practically the same means as the first. Apparently William accepted the advice of his lieutenants who believed that a second calamity was unlikely. He knew only too well that the task was a formidable one and while disinclined to tempt fate, his superstitious nature succumbed to the advice of his officers who exhorted him to enlist the services of a wellknown witch. This he had great cause to regret. Reinforced and replenished with suitable equipment and engines of war the royal army made ready to storm the Isle. The King commanded that a great store of timber be set up for the construction of the new causeway. The chronicler tells us that local fishermen were pressed to assist and that they brought their boats to a place called Cotinglade (Cottenham?) with materials to build the causeway (or repair the existing one). He also recounts that Hereward was not without knowledge of this plan and as soon as the materials had been collected together in large quantities, he took the opportunity of setting fire to the pile.

This prompted the King to order a strict watch night and day. The operation proceeded apparently without further mishap. Meanwhile the besieged islanders, lacking nothing and excelling in cunning, noted carefully the Normans' progress and accordingly devised counter plans. Timbers, roped together and protected by stretched skins were placed by the Norman engineers upon the morass to form a bailey-type bridge which took a week to build. On the eighth day only a short distance remained to be bridged and the Royal army was given positions along the causeway. The witch uttered incantations from a wooden tower near the business end of the causeway and everything was ready for the assault. Then, without warning, the reeds and bracken flanking the causeway burst into flame, ignited by men from the Isle hidden behind bulwarks and occupying concealed positions in the marsh. Individuals were picked off by archers and most of the Norman soldiers were engulfed in a sea of scorching flame and wreathed by dense smoke. The witch, we are told, fell from her exalted position and broke her neck. A roll call revealed an appalling loss of life and the King, mixing with survivors that had formed the reserves was heard to lament the loss of so many fine men. He had reluctantly consented to the plan against his better judgement and he criticised those advisers that had persuaded him to carry out the action a second time.

It would seem that a large number of Norman Knights followed by men-at-arms were almost at the point of storming the Isle defences which had been erected opposite the approaching bridgework. Another sizeable force stood by further to the rear ready to reinforce the forward "commandos" on the bridgehead. In this way no more weight than necessary would be placed on the secured timbers of the causeway with its degrees of instability as had happened on the previous occasion. The army had the support of "engines", probably mangons or trebuchets for hurling rocks and stones. After the fires had been started the soldiers panicked, having no means of egress with marsh on each side and they were at the mercy of concealed archers. The fire extended nearly half the length of the causeway parts which probably blazed and few men from the forward position would escape. Most were proved fighters, Knights, chosen to go first for the honour and with the King's promise of lands. Cut off by the inferno they perished on the causeway, pierced and drowned, dragged down by the marsh by the weight of their weapons and coats of mail-hauberks made of leather or linen on which were sewn flat rings of iron. In true Norman tradition they carried metal shields reaching as high as a man's shoulder, with a rounded top and pointed at the base. The men-at-arms, usually foot soldiers, wore hauberks and conical helmets and were armed with javelins. The second force one supposes mainly men-at-arms, according to the chronicler were more fortunate, withdrawing along the unaffected part of the causeway and from a safe distance witnessed their comrades dying helplessly in the raging reed fires. This is the only account of substance concerning what was a major attempt to take the Isle by force.

When Ely's monks capitulated, it is said that Hereward spent a little while in the temporary security of the "Wide Sea" which lay near the Welle Stream (the present River Nene, old course) which flows through March and Upwell. (The name Waldersea between March and Wisbech may have historical links with this "Sea"). Hotly pursued, Hereward left the Fens and continued to resist the Normans, apparently enjoying a famous victory against soldiers from several provinces, the battle taking place presumably in a heavily wooded area not very far from Peterborough. William The Conqueror secured the Fen region by erecting a substantial castle at Wisbech, over looking the estuaries of the River Wyse and River Ouse, the latter allowing access to the Isle of Ely. Tradition has it that Wisbech castle was built in 1071, the year when the rebellion was suppressed. Oddly, Domesday (1086) makes no mention of it. Did the Normans occupy an already existing earthwork on a temporary basis until a more substantial building came into existence after 1086?

Ancient documents testify to these events of over nine centuries ago. In 1607 Camden wrote of the erection of stockades on the edges of the Fens. Near Aldreth.."there is an open passage into the Isle of Ely and to this day there is a rampart nigh Audrey, not high but very large, called Belsar's Hill". Further reference to the King's chief man is evidenced in a manuscript entitled "A Story found in the Isle of Ely", (British Museum). In it is written "...Belasius the Norman was placed at Ely with a monk named Oswald." ("II, Belasius Preses Militum versus Ely, cum Othwaldo monacho..."). The soldier was second in order among 40 Norman Knights therein mentioned, these placed with as many monks. It is a clear indication to the period immediately following cessation of hostilities on and around the Isle of Ely, a time when the Church at Ely pleaded for the restoration of its rights and privileges, these granted eventually.

The Conqueror free at last from Ely's threat to the throne, exerted his authority very forcibly and the vanquished, notably the Church were not allowed to forget. It was not, however, the end of Hereward and if ancient manuscripts can be believed, he lived to fight another day. The historic battleground in the Fens was a favourite debating point in the centuries which followed. An historian wrote: "We endured the violent threat of the Normans seven (?) years until such times as Belasius, general of the King's army, in the service of whome certain hills at the south end of Aldreth Causeway were built for the safety of the armies took their name which we now, by corrupt speech, call Belsar's Hills, getting a great company of boats, passed the waters on a soddayn and set us at our wits end . . ." (MS Tiberius, Brit. Mus.).

The Saxon hierarchy, exhausted after a courageous and prolonged struggle for freedom upheld in the north, west and finally at Ely, bowed out with dignity and a new and dramatic epoch began. The insurgents derived some satisfaction knowing that, in partnership with the forboding environment they had effectively tied down much, if not all of one of the acknowledged finest armies of that era. Defeat came not as a direct military victory, but sadly, yet wisely, through submission by a despairing Church which had armed its monks and encouraged them to fight alongside professional men. From the outset the Church had seen fit to succour the insurgents in a bid to prevent the French from seizing English establishments that it might retain its ancient privileges and rights, only to give way when threatened with the prospect of losing them.

Hereward was a born leader in the military sense. His place was on the battlefield and directing guerrilla campaigns. He presented his opponents with profound problems but his valour and fair mindedness evoked begrudging admiration. Hereward was recognised for his ability to deploy men strategically in a manner centuries after his time.

The role of the man, his faults and fame, were put down on parchment by a churchman an historian for his time. Preserved for centuries in Peterborough Cathedral library the manuscript tells of the exploits of Hereward the Saxon - "the last of the true English."

THE FENS in full flood. Islands, surrounded by meres and marsh afforded ideal protection for the farming population and marshes provided abundant fish and fowl. (Photo: T. Bevis)

ALDRETH CAUSEWAY, ancient entry into the Isle of Ely and traditional site of William The First's disastrous attempt to subjugate the island. Belsar's Hill, an earthwork two miles distant at Willingham is said to have accommodated part of the Norman army. (Photo: T. Bevis)

STUNTNEY CAUSEWAY, built in the 12th century for the benefit of pilgrims, alternative site of the Conqueror's attempt to overcome resistance. Ancient weapons have been discovered in the vicinity. (Photo: T. Bevis)

9

ELY CATHEDRAL, commenced by Abbot Simeon about 15 years after the monks' submission to the King. In the refectory of the Saxon monastery Hereward dined with other nobles and monks, the latter trained to fight as soldiers. (Photo: T. Bevis)

WITCHFORD CHURCH. At this village Ely's monks met the displeased King. He fined them 700 marks and they were made to support 40 Norman knights as a penalty for their part in the siege. (Photo: T. Bevis)

De Gestis Herwardi Saxonis

(The Exploits of Hereward The Saxon)

I. (Addressed to the Abbot)
Here begins the preface of a certain work concerning the exploits of Hereward the renowned Knight.
Some of us desiring to learn of the deeds of the noble Hereward, an Englishman, and his renowned men, and to hear of his generous actions and doings, the brethren of your house have helped us by enquiring if any man had left anything in writing about so great a man in the place where he once lived. For when we declared that we had heard in a certain place that a short account had been written about him in English, straight-away you sought the whereabouts of that writing and before long translated into Latin, adding also the things which we had heard from our own people with whom he (Hereward) was well known, living nobly as a soldier.

Desiring, therefore, to satisfy your desires we enquired in many places, and yet found nothing except a few scattered leaves, partly rotten by damp, and decayed and partly damaged by tearing. When the pen had been put to its task we have with difficulty extracted from it his descent from his parents and his character among other things; that is to say the early achievements of the very famous outlaw Hereward, edited in English by Leofric the Deacon, his priest at Bourne. For the intention of this well known priest was to collect all the acts of the famous warriors from stories, or from trustworthy narration, for the edification of his hearers, and for their remembrance to commit them to the English language. And although insufficiently skilled in this, or rather incompetent to decipher what is obliterated of the unfamiliar language, we have gathered concerning Hereward on his return to that place and to his ancestral home where he had found his brother murdered. We leave this material, written in rude style, to your care and to the zeal of some man's trained ability to be interpreted in simpler and plainer language.

We have been able to decipher nothing further than this, ever hoping for greater results but as yet finding nothing thoroughly. For they, deluded for a long time, derived hope from others who said that in a place there is a great book of his exploits from the beginning, found nothing of what they had been led to expect, although they sent to the place. We eventually abandoned the search completely and put away the work we had begun. But some of our men did not want us to do this, and unexpectedly you kindly directed that at least the commencement should not be denied you. It was then an object of care to us, for want of great ability that you might see our incomplete work, and take up the pen once more and again to present to you a little book in the manner of a history, concerning these things which we have heard from our own men and from some of his (Hereward's) with whom they had associated from the beginning of his career and were in many ways his comrades. We have seen some of these men, tall in stature and huge and of exceeding courage, and you yourselves have seen also two men conspicuous for their form as you yourself told us, namely Siwate, Bother of St. Edmunds, and Leofric Niger, his Knights, although injured by enemies, being bereft of some members by trickery, through envy. Indeed of these and others, proved and seen, it is given to you to understand of what valour their lord was, and how much greater were the things that he did what they reported of him. We think it will encourage noble deeds and induce liberality to know Hereward, who he was, and to hear of his achievements and deeds, and especially to those who are desirous of living the life of a soldier. Wherefore we advise you, give attention and you who the more diligently strive to hear the deeds of brave men, apply your minds to hear diligently the account of so great a man: for he trusting neither in fortification, nor in garrison, but in himself, alone with his men waged war against Kingdoms and Kings, and fought against princes and tyrants, some of whom he conquered. Concerning which things, beginning with his parents, everything has been inserted by chapters, so that what is here distinctly set down may be easily remembered.

II. Of what parents Hereward was born and how from his boyhood he increased in the splendour of his deeds, and why he was driven forth by his father and country; accordingly he was surnamed "The Outlaw".

Of the nations of the English many very mighty men are recorded, and Hereward the Outlaw is esteemed most distinguished and a famous Knight with the more famous. His father was Leofric of Bourne, grandson of Earl Radulf surnamed Scabre; his mother was Aediva, great-great-grand-daughter of Duke Oslac, most nobly descended by both parents. He was as a boy remarkable for his figure and comely in aspect, very beautiful from his yellow hair, and with large grey eyes, the right eye slightly different in colour to the left; but he was stern of feature and somewhat stout, from the great sturdiness of his limbs, but very active for his moderate stature, and in all his limbs was found a complete vigour. There was in him also from his youth much grace and strength of body; and from practice of this when a young man the character of his valour showed him a perfect man, and he was excellently endowed in all things with the grace of courage and valour of mind. As regards liberality he was from his father's possessions and his own, bountiful and most liberal, giving relief to all in need. Although cruel in act, and severe in play, readily stirring up quarrels among those of his own age, and often exciting contests among his elders in cities and villages; leaving none equal to himself in deeds of daring and pursuit of brave actions, not even among his elders.

While youthfully developing and progressing in courage from day to day, and excelling in manly deeds, at times he spared no-one whom he knew to be at all a rival in courage or in fighting. For these reasons he very often stirred up sedition among the populace and tumult among the ordinary people. By this he made his father opposed to him and his parents very ungracious. Because of his deeds of courage and boldness they were daily contending with their friends and neighbours and amongst the country folk who behaved like enemies and tyrants because of him, almost always protecting their son when returning from sport or fighting with drawn swords and arms. At length, his father, unable to endure this, drove him from his presence. Nor then, indeed did he keep quite, but taking with him those of his own age when his father was away on his estates, he sometimes preceded him and distributed his goods amongst his own friends and supporters, even appointing in some of his father's possessions stewards and servants of his own, to supply corn to his men. His father begged King Edward that he might be banished, making known all the harm he had committed against his parents, and against the country and people. This was done. From then on he was known as the Outlaw, being driven from his father and country in the 18th year of his age.

III. How Hereward slew a great bear by which deed he earned a position amongst the Knights with whom he was staying.

When Gisebritus of Gant heard of this, namely his banishment, he sent for him, for Hereward was godson of that rich man. He set out beyond Northumberland and came to him, abandoning his own province and paternal inheritance, with one servant, Martin Lightfoot. After he had been there a short time an occurrence worthy of praise took place. The rich man had a custom at Easter, Pentecost and Christmas to test the strength and courage of the young men who were waiting for the belt and arms of Knighthood by leading savage beasts from cages. Hereward had associated himself with these young men at the commencement of his visit, namely at Christmas, and he asked that he might be allowed to attack one of the wild beasts, or at least a very large bear which was there, which men said was the offspring of a famous Norwegian bear, its head and feet in shapes of perfect monstrosity, having the sense of a man and understanding the speech of man, and skilled in war, whose sire is reported to have ravished a girl in the woods and to have become by her father of Biernus, King of Norway. Hereward could not obtain permission, the lord perceiving the bravery of the young man, but fearing for his youthfulness.

On the next day the beast broke away from its chains and rushed forth from the bars of its cage, renting and slaying every living thing it could reach. When the lord heard of the circumstances, he ordered his soldiers to get ready and attack it with lances, adding that it could not possibly be taken alive. Meanwhile Hereward came across the blood-stained beast as he was returning to the lord's chamber, because of the alarmed people and lord's wife and daughters and the women, frightened, had fled. The beast immediately wanted to rush upon him. But Hereward anticipated it and drove his sword through its head down to the shoulder blades. Leaving the blade there he took up the beast in his arms and held it out to those that followed. They were much amazed. Truly he earned no little favour with his lord and lady, as well as grievious hate and envy with the Knights and boys of the house. Therefore by reason of this deed he obtained position and honour with the Knights, although at the time he did not wish to become a Knight until he had made better trial of his valour and courage.

And so the countryfolk extolled him and the women and girls used to sing about him in their dances, which grieved his enemies; and because he daily increased, as in grace and age, so also in the virtues of courage and hardihood. None equalled him in the chase and hunting, nor in games enjoyed by the common people or gentlefolk. Therefore, they sought for a fitting time and place of killing him. When on a certain day their lord was by chance absent, hunting in the woods, the Knights of the household attempted to slay him with a javelin hurled by one well-known to him and whom, only three days before Hereward had delivered from death when the man had been taken by enemies. Having learned this plot just in time through his servant, Hereward pierced with his lance the man who was in the act of throwing the javelin at him. Having disclosed this to his lady, and desiring to avoid similar events, he went away. She in tears, entreated him at least to wait for the lord's return, or for the death of their sick son, and said that if he did not leave he should be their adopted son and heir. But Hereward would not grant her request.

IV. How Hereward overcame a certain tyrant, and took his famous sword.

From this place Hereward went to a certain Prince of Cornwall, called Alef, where he found a most wicked and very haughty man, Ulcus Ferreus (Iron Sore) by name, who because of his wonderful courage, expected to win the very fair daughter of the Prince. This man from the nation of the Scots and Picts, was esteemed a very brave warrior, as though there could be none to compare with him in any nation. For wherever he was staying, many used to flock to him, as to some great sight for the sake of hearing of his achievements; and he used readily, though untruly, to din these things into the ears of his hearers, boasting that no one man, not even two or three, could be a match for him. As he often did this before the Royal Family and before the Prince himself, he one day grossly abused the nation of the English, saying the English were without the virtue of strength, and worth nothing in war, declaring that he had with one blow killed three men out of a number, on a certain occasion. Indignant at this, Hereward in derision, before them all, answered: "Since you have imagined in your mind those three men who you declare were slain by you, and have begotten those sons not of a mother but of your own heart, it is quite right they should be slain by one blow of your mouth." At this his future wife, the daughter of the aforesaid King, was dissolved into laughter. This greatly offended the tyrant, and he straightaway threatened Hereward, "In truth you should soon lie slain by my own hands, save only for the presence of the lord." To whom Hereward replied, "See that so sturdy a Knight as you boast yourself to be does not use craft against a young man. Otherwise if you shall without craft pursue him of whom you speak, you will always find me ready, so that your triumph, if it comes, may be the more glorious." He then, mindful of his words by chance met Hereward, when he was unarmed, in a neighbouring grove of the lord. "Lo", said the tyrant at once, "now is the time for avenging myself on my enemy. Today from a gift of your hair, she shall be dissolved in laughter or in sorrow, who once was pleased at the insolence of your words, and praised your head of hair and face, and the arrogance of your reply." Hereward answered, "For one well provided with arms and strength to crush the helpless, is no glory to a man of renown; but yet if I fall, let your generosity, if you have any, grant me the space of one hour, that I may give my property to the priest to bestow upon the poor, and then I will come back." With an oath the man gave his assent and promised to reveal the affair to nobody.

So Hereward departed and armed himself. Having soon returned at the first signal of onset pierced his javelin into the tyrant's thighs and struggling together for a time they smote one another. Then the young man (Hereward) by advance and attack avoided the blows and kept falling back and retreating often inflicting blows not expected or open. But when the abominable man saw the spirit of the youth, he strove to grasp him with his hands for he was stronger and much taller. But always Hereward avoided him, until as he was bending down rather incautiously Hereward thrust his sword into his groin just beneath his breast-plate. Then, drenched in blood, feeling that death was near, the tyrant said, "Alas! alas! see how I, so very strong, trusting in my strength, from lack of caution lie overthrown by a crafty boy! Oh if that blade were now at hand, which I later handed to my future spouse, with which I overcame such mighty men, if fortune befriended me, with one blow half-dead as I am I would at least avenge myself - that blade which I received from fighting with a certain tyrant." The boys of the house, hearing the noise of arms ran to the spot, then told of the affair to their lord, who sent armed men thither to separate them, fearing that Hereward would be killed. When they arrived they found to their surprise, the tyrant dead. Upon this Hereward was apprehended, because the tyrant was already spoken of as the prince's son-in-law. They took him to the prince. Then immediately the whole of that hostile nation desired to rise against Hereward, saying that their mightiest man had been slain by trickery. But the prince himself in order that Hereward be saved, restrained them, and kept him in custody, as though intending to decide what should be done about him. The prince's daughter, greatly delighted at what had happened, for she had greatly dreaded that terrible and mis-shapen man, with great care ministered to Hereward, and in the end, having presented him with gifts and the aforesaid sword which the tyrant had given to her, caused him to leave in secret, desiring him to remember her, and giving him marks and token to the son of the King of Ireland, informing him by letter how her enemy had been slain by Hereward.

V. Of the war which took place in Ireland, and how Hereward slew the leader of the opposite army with seven comrades in the midst of his men.

When these things were known, Hereward was honourably received by the King of Ireland's son, and they made him remain with them for several days, although he was unwilling, because he wished after delivering his message to return to his father's house and to his widowed mother. He had found two very distinguished men, Siward the White and Siward the Red, sons of his own uncle, who told him that his father was dead and that his mother was by herself in the inheritance consigned to him. When he had been there a little while it was announced to the King that a war against the Duke of Munster was imminent. On an appointed day all the adherants of the King in the neighbourhood begged and entreated Hereward with his men to take part in the battle and to help them, since they had heard many instances of his bravery, and now even in the short time he had been with them they themselves had discovered very many things worth relating of him. Therefore Hereward complying with their entreaties and with his elders enthusiastically arranged and disposed all things in preparation for the war, and even in the very day of battle. He drew up the lines and led them, while seven of his comrades were assigned the duty of attacking the leader of the opposing army in the midst of his men, should the battle be doubtful, and if their forces were at all giving way.

This they did: in the midst of the enemy's wedges, killing to the right and left, they made their way up to the leader's tent, and found him lying down at the entrance with two old men Hereward quickly explained his appearance and told him he must yield and give honour to his lord, or else he must know that they would fall upon him. However, he did not consent for he knew his men were fighting bravely, and defending himself with his own hand he protected himself for a short time, after the two old men had been killed, shouting for help as he was surrounded by enemies. Then Hereward attacked and slew him while others guarded the entrance of the tent. They then returned through the cohort, having the leader's sword for a signal and a trumpet, for they had closely surrounded them and had laid low one of their men, namely the King's grandson, in their retreat being almost overwhelmed, having lost two comrades and both of Hereward's nephews were grieviously wounded. At length they reached their allies and sounded the leaders trumpet at which in great alarm the enemy retreated. From this the name of Hereward throughout the Kingdom was highly praised, and his fame among the neighbouring tribes increased daily. Many very mighty men and sons o powerful men, hearing the news, hastened to him to be instructed in arms and courtesy Hereward himself next with the King's son, having got together a band of soldiers, subdued the whole place and land that was opposed to the King, as well as his enemies in the neighbourhood in the space of a year. The valour of his ancestors could not approach that o Hereward.

VI. How Hereward in disguise was sent by his lord to a wedding, where he achieved notable action, in killing the bridegroom, and carrying off the bride and conveying her to his lord.

While in a remote part of the land they were leading their band against Cornwall, a messenger from the King of Cornwall's daughter, met them with this message: "Alas! alas! why is it that you are so long unmindful of your hand maiden? Could I ever have had this opinion of you, that you would deceive a young girl? I am delivered into the hands of a petty prince of Ireland under your very eyes, and his son is marrying me against my will, though I am in love with you. Oh that I in this emergency might experience the energy you display towards others! For otherwise that faith which I once gave to the noble son of the King of Ireland, I shall always cherish in my mind, should I not be able to escape. If you abandon your honour like a barbarian and not save a girl for her betrothed, remember I pray you what dealings I have had with you." Having read this message the King's son immediately sent to the father of the girl's ambassadors, some forty men with military equipment with two leaders, charging him to remember the former bargain, how his daughter was betrothed to him: or else he must realise that he would attack with arms both himself and the man that took his daughter, and get her wherever she was married.

Hereward by another road undertook the journey with three companions, having disguised himself with ointment and changed his yellow hair to black and his youthful beard to a red colour. At length they arrived at the place and found the messengers of the King's son in custody, and the intended son-in-law of the Cornish prince ready to depart the following day to his own possessions with his bride. Immediately Hereward went in to see the wedding, saying that he was a stranger from a far away place and was going into the service of a certain nobleman from the west of their land. Although late he was received into the marriage party and welcomed by the guests. He took his seat with his men at the end of the table, choosing the lowest seat. The King's daughter observed this and his familiar form but was very astonished at his complexion. Then, remembering the estimable Hereward whom she had lately freed from prison, and had sent to the son of the King of Ireland, she wept, and from recollection of him sent him a small dish on a tray, saying : "Since he is a stranger and of unknown dignity, and is resting at the end of the table let him accept this present with its contents that he may not abuse the bridegroom or the young bride in a foreign country, or denounce them at another wedding."

Then the attendant delivered the tray to Hereward, who understanding the message laid hold of the dish and squeezed the fingers of the attendant's hands causing the blood to flow from beneath his nails. Accordingly, those present abused him excessively and called him diabolical and disorderly, and that he ought not to share the banquet. Hereward answered them with reference to what was passing in his mind: "I will neither join in the joy of the banquet nor partake of the pleasures of the wedding until I can wait upon you as you do now upon me." On being informed of this the princess more and more kept asking herself who he was, and revealed the affair to her nurse, if by chance she could find out if it were Hereward or his brother. On seeing him she immediately declared that it was indeed Hereward with the colour of his hair changed, but she advised her to make sure. After dinner, the bride in royal dress, as was the practice of the province, went forth with her damsels to offer drink to the guests and servants of her parents. As she left her fathers house, she was preceded by a harpist and while he played she offered a cup to each person, this being a peculiar and novel piece of humour in those places.

One of the damsels offered Hereward a cup filled with wine, while the harpist stood nearby, but Hereward would not accept it from the hand of a woman, because he and the King of Ireland's son had made a vow to take nothing before they received from the hand of the prince's daughter something long desired. This slight to the cup bearer antagonised the guests, and the jester described the affair with vehement feeling to his mistress, while she was still offering the cup to the guests. Then she drew near to Hereward and offered him the cup, standing directly before him, for a glance of her eyes immediately recognised him and she knew by the shape of his limbs that it was Hereward himself. She immediately placed a ring from her own hand into the fold of his garments, directing that he should for the future be excused as being unacquainted with their customs. The jester wandered everywhere and would not rest, but as often as he passed declared that the man who at a banquet would despise the cup bearer with his cup was not worthy to strike the lyre. Hereward, stirred to anger at the jester's remarks, made answer which the fool spread around, saying that if he would give him the opportunity he would better discharge that duty than himself. The jester with indignation, as though he alone were skilled in the art, placed the harp in Hereward's arms. Taking it, Hereward most skilfully struck the strings, and produced sounds and strains to the admiration of all, while the other was quite frightened at the occurrence and kept trying to take back the harp from his hands. But the guests judged him worthy of a present and that meanwhile he should have an attendant.

As he persisted in offering him drink, in order it seemed that he should not be recognised, he acquiesed in various ways singing with the harp. He sang with different tones at one time by himself, at another time with two others of his own kind after the manner of the Girvii, (Fenmen). Whereupon all were greatly delighted, and he obtained from the bride a beautiful cloak as a reward, and the bridegroom whatever he liked to ask for except his wife and his land. Hereward asked that the messengers of the King of Ireland's son should be immediately set free. When it had been decided to grant this request, a certain spokesman, jealous of the players, interrupted the lord, saying: "This man is one of those wicked messengers and has come here to spy upon your house, or rather to mock you, leading off your enemies by means of this most contemptible sport, or because they had not the strength, the scoffer, artful in skill, as well as in mockery, may obtain some of them". This was a good speech in the speaker's eyes, and he bid his listeners to watch Hereward - "that vile fellow" cautiously, for if he were apprehended at once there would probably be a tumult at the banquet, as he intended to go the following day with the messengers of the King of Ireland's son to the show, while he himself returned with the bride to his own home. He added that all these men ought to be deprived of their right eyes, and so dismissed.

Now Hereward had previously learned of these things from the King's daughter and he took counsel for his escape. Calling his companions he strove to anticipate his enemies because his men had been seized. He lay hidden in a nearby grove, near some water, which surrounds a part of that Kingdom and forms a boundary, awaiting their arrival and the passage of a number of men that preceded them. When almost all had crossed and the prisoners had been bound so that once across the river the messengers might be deprived of their eyes, Hereward leapt with his companions from his hiding place and hurled his javelin at the tyrant, while his men loosened the bonds of those that were bound, whereby the rescuers soon had considerable numbers. At length, Hereward, mounting the tyrant's horse led away that man's bride and with his companions hurried to meet the King of Ireland's son with his army which was directed to assist. After a space of three days, all the cavalry being tired out, except the tyrant's horse upon which was seated the young lady, and many of Hereward's companions, half dead with heat and hunger and the rigours of the retreat, they arrived in silence at the royal camp in the middle of the night. The prince, heartily congratulated them, and married the lady.

VII. How Hereward endured shipwreck on his return from Ireland, and in Flanders being a second time overwhelmed by a storm he there changed his name.

Hereward had a great desire to visit his dependants and parents and obtained from the King two ships fitted out with arms and all naval equipment, although the aged King resented him going and would rather that Hereward stay in the country and take one of his grand-daughters in marriage or the daughter of any rich man living in Ireland that he approved of. Hereward declined these offers. Having embarked he was driven by a storm to the Orkneys, and from there a hurricane drove the ship to Flanders, thus for a second time he suffered shipwreck, on that occasion near Bertinum. Manascar, the Count of that land and the nobles of that country, sending men to the place, led them out that all might be seen, for he regarded the newcomers as precursors of some army, or rather spies. When they saw the ship's equipment and the splendid men it contained and how well they were armed, the Count's representatives asked Hereward who he was, his country and the reason of his arrival. Hereward replied that he was of the race of the English, and that perchance it was his intention to serve as a soldier in many places and lands. That he was going to do business and would pursue any profession that fortune might assign to him that his name was Harold and he had been driven to those regions by a storm from Ireland. It was off Flanders he had been

16

shipwrecked. Hereward had given orders that his men must not utter his real name or disclose his rank or dignity. At length the Count, doubting who he was and where he came from, ordered Hereward and his men to be kept in honourable custody for a time.

VIII. Of Hereward's first fighting in Flanders by which and from his daily deeds of valour, he was at length discovered, which prompted much enquiry as to who such a man could be, and where he came from.

The Count of Flanders was at war with the neighbouring Count of Ginnes when his men daily proceeded to single combats in front of the castles and farms in the campaign. Hereward anxiously implored him to allow him to go out with them for one day. At length he obtained permission. As he was well trained in arms and management of war he therefore acted with prudence on the day. Far from the company a soldier was overthrown by another and Hereward defended him, then brought him back, killing four men who attacked him, to the admiration of all for they supposed that both had been taken prisoners. From this, great account was made of him in the palace of the prince and he was reckoned one of their strongest men and from that time Hereward went out and returned with them, daily accomplishing fresh deeds of valour in fight.

Now the prince of the land was much in doubt as to who or what or of what country such a man could be, and he enquired of his foreigners and merchants for news concerning him: if by chance his name (falsely Harold) or fame were known in any distant land. It was not long before the much desired information was given. Someone said that three years before he had seen such a man in Ireland, like him in valour and appearance and that he had heard many things about him and that he was called by name, Hereward. Having discovered this, the Count and his only son questioned Hereward as to the object of his deceit and asked him his name and country and dignity and family, assuring him with an oath that he would regard him as a very dear son. At length Hereward admitted that the information concerning him was true, and told them his name and where he came from, how being driven forth by his father he had gone first to Cornwall and afterwards to Ireland, and he explained the reason of his arrival at that place.

IX. How Hereward overcame a famous soldier, and led him safe and sound to his companions.

There was occasionally present in the party of the enemy a grandson of the Count of Ginnes, by name Hoibrictus, a Knight glorious for courage and well versed in the knowledge of warfare, who was accounted in the army like a lion among a flock for bravery. By himself one day, Hereward came upon this man beyond his company. Without recognising one another, out of excessive valour, they enthusiastically clashed together, and at the first onset their lances were broken. Then they attacked each other with swords, and Hereward dealt his opponent an astounding blow beneath the ear. Although many rushed to his assistance, Hereward, evading them all, took him up in his arms and carried him to his companions despite the man recovering his senses and striving to escape. The Count of Ginnes wondered at this, and was alarmed and grieved because of the downfall of his grandson, a renowned soldier. On the following day he offered due honour and service to his prince and sent presents and hostages. For he had heard of the fame of Hereward, so worthy of praise, and what he had done in Ireland and Cornwall. And now he had seen his bravery.

X. How Hereward is beloved by a certain girl, for whose sake he went forth to combat, and there with his men proved victorious.

At that time there lived at Saint Admarus a young lady noble and beautiful, much devoted to liberal knowledge and skilled in mechanical arts. She was called Turfrida. She fell in love with Hereward, having heard of his achievements, and she displayed many of her accomplishments, as they say, for love of him, and by so doing secured her his affection for herself. But another man of the neighbourhood was in love with her. He was a famous soldier and grandson of a very powerful man of Saint Walericus. So in love was he that he threatened some mischief, or even death, to Hereward. When Hereward was going to the contests which are held at the Bridges and Pictavia, together with the recruits of his lord, and was taking them to make their first attempt at such competitions, quite unawares he came across his adversary in company with his men, and advancing in the middle of his troops, carrying a token from a girl's chaplet, for his sweetheart's sake, as though he had accomplished his warfare. On seeing him Hereward immediately advanced upon him, and at the first onslaught overthrew him and took away his token and horse.

Hereward sent this to the young lady, and other tokens on his own part, there being still three not overcome by him, and several by his fellow soldiers, while he was always accompanying and protecting each one. And so being especially honoured with his men, by reason of his victory, above all, he confesses to his comrades that he is greatly in love with the aforesaid young lady, but ingnorant of how he could approach her, dreading the snares of his many foes. Then he made his way to her with very few of his companions, directing that his absence should be made known to none.

But Hereward's departure to this meeting and the cause of his coming was not concealed from his rival, who arranged ambushes in many places, with robbers and malefactors to meet him. Of these one day 17 out of 40 robbers were withdrawn, and Hereward killed 25 of those who attacked him, then continued his journey. At last, though pressed by very many rascals on the road, he arrived at his destination and said that he was a messenger of Hereward's and indeed his nephew, namely Siward the White, bringing a message and presents from his master to her, who in great delight immediately kissed him. But looking earnestly at the expression of his eyes, and from his comely face, and golden hair and the vigour of his body, she at last recognised him. Immediately she burst forth in these words :"Lo! I embrace in my arms the most excellent of all men, and see with my eyes the most renowned soldier, and now, though late, I am in the presence of the man most desired."

Hereward repudiated the suggestion and told her she was mistaken. But she, after strictly enquiring from him as to some personal tokens and scars that indicated slight wounds, maintained on the contrary that he was her most beloved Hereward. At this he was overcome and admitted the truth. While this was discussed in private, she led him away to the inside of the house and showed him all her father's riches in gold and silver, or of other material, belonging to her mother, and also a corselet of excessive lightness and very fine work, and much brighter and purer than any steel or iron, and a helmet of similar beauty and strength, adding about them, "There have been many rich and powerful men that have enquired about these, where they are, and offering gifts for their production, desiring to get them for themselves by trickery or threats, or force, or money, or by any artifice they could: but I have kept them hitherto of my forefather's possessions, ever the dearest possessions of my forefather and grandfather, and father, that I might present them to my betrothed. And now of all men I favour you for the suitable valour of your courage and for your bravery, and it is very agreeable and right for me that you should tell a suitable lover if you are glad of the gift. For I am willing in my own person to undergo anything, should anything surpass them in steel or metal."

Greatly delighted, Hereward thanked her for the gifts, and they gave each other pledges of fidelity. At last he returned to his fellow soldiers who were waiting for him. The same night, in the guest house, quite unawares Hereward encountered a foe, one of the attendants of his rival. In the silence of the night this man went to attack Hereward with an axe while he was asleep. As it happened he turned round from his bed, wide awake and struck the assailant on to the bedclothes. All his companions were aroused and seized the man. When they had discovered where he had come from and of his master, they cut off his right hand. From that time, Hereward rested near his own bed, or else to lie in the bed of one of his men situated in a different place. On that night he arrived at his lord's, with his companions. His lord congratulated them, for he had heard all about the affair, and he forthright enriched them with rewards and honours. But Hereward would accept nothing, till he should demand and receive the young lady with her lands.

XI. Hereward with a certain leader was sent to Scaldemariland with an army, and overcame the opposing army.

The Count of Flanders had sent ambassadors into Scaldemariland for tribute long overdue, and for the rating of the land. About this time in that land these messengers were reported to have been deprived of one eye, and to have had the left foot cut off. It seemed opportune therefore to the Prince and his followers to send Hereward to that region with an army and its general, that fitting justice be handed out to those that had done these things, or alternatively to punish the enemy severely. Although a difficult assignment, Hereward gladly undertook it. With a fleet in their train they arrived at the place with very favourable weather and a prosperous wind. It was not long before they were confronted with a great multitude of the enemy, who threatened to overwhelm them with a great show of javelins, or to make prisoners of them and enslave them. At this the army was greatly alarmed and wanted to retreat.

Hereward inspired the waverers in light-hearted fashion, declaring that in their experience of war they must have no fear despite the numerical advantages of the enemy which were ill arranged and audacious: for this was the confidence of rashness and the arrogance of the enemy's own forthcoming destruction. At this the army was greatly encouraged and it stood up the more eagerly, for the destruction of those that threatened it. Of the forty ships, four together with a large number of men took places at the rear, so that if some fell others might take their place. Hereward demanded that while others attacked, he would have the central position so that the youths and boys might test their strength, or that should they be exasperated by the fight, they could be provoked into the battle or rather in such a way they might try their inferior valour in war before they proceeded to greater deeds.

As Hereward deployed his men, the enemy perceived it with joy, confiding in their strength, and they set one man in the middle, against whom Hereward advanced. When this man was overthrown he was replaced with another and others, one after the other, but none could survive against Hereward, for though armed they knew not how to defend themselves, nor how to protect with their arms their awkward bodies. Declaring that he mocked them, and thinking him to be a magician, all endeavoured to rush on him at once, Hereward suddenly turned round to his companions and found that they were uncautiously separated behind him, but he got them within reach, whereby his enemies were at length overcome.

XII. Of the second war at Scaldemariland and how that nation advanced to the battle and how they were armed; and how Hereward arranged his army against them.

Immediately all that dangerous nation and outrageous people recruited the whole population from all sides of the island to come together and they ravaged and laid waste their borders over a period of fourteen days, lest being so insecure they should be driven out, or rather become subject in that time to foreigners, like the English people to the French; nor had they heard a false report. Having gathered all together into one place by the Flanders army, orders were given that the invading army be cut off, and all the men who had come hither might have their lives spared, but would lose everything else except a few ships and their tackling. They were to deliver up besides Robert, the leader of the army, and Hereward the master of the soldiers, and the tribunes of the companies, that these men be put to death in the place of all others. For they had brought to the same place waggons and chariots so as to convey away their possessions and arms. Seeing this, and at Hereward's suggestion, they burned all their chariots and vehicles in front of the opposing side's ambassadors and would have ordered these people to be cast into the flames themselves, had it not been that the rights of intermediaries would seem to be broken, and the privilege of an embassy to be violated. Therefore, Hereward persuaded the army and its officers that these ambassadors should be detained for a while, either by force or cajolery. Meanwhile the rest should prepare for fighting and arrange their lines, appointing to each line a leader, an appointed work and a superintendent. All this, in the event, proved to be successful, because the enemy, imprudent and inexperienced, seeing some messengers heavily laden with presents, and eagerly coveting such things, made their way to them in great numbers, each anxious to secure the best things before others.

Three hundred picked soldiers under Hereward encountered these as they were running in front of the army to reconnoitre and made no small slaughter of them, pursuing some right up to the tents of their comrades. Everyone was completely astounded and realised that they had been taken unawares. Accordingly with great anger and supreme indignation, they advanced ready for battle, vowing that they would not leave a single man alive. They carried with them these arms: coats of felt dipped in pitch and resin and incense, or tunics strongly made of leather, and in their hands spears studded with nails and twisted for thrusting and pulling way, or for striking, and with three of four squared javelins for throwing. Between each couple so armed, another soldier bore a sword or an axe, bearing also a shield before the couple. The enemy were great in number, but badly arranged. The Flemish army's leader and Hereward the master of the soldiers, seeing the enemy go down into the valley, drew up their army against them on the heights. When they came together as little by little others came against them, they retreated, since they wished to draw the enemy away from their tents, and having gone some distance from their quarters, the men of Flanders ceased to withdraw, turned and stood to battle. Hereward with 1,000 horse soldiers and 600 other armed men killed the enemy guarding their camp, then led his force to the rear of the men of Scaldemariland, where he came upon them all almost unarmed. Being wholly unable to defend themselves they were routed.

Those of the enemy in the front lines, realising this unexpected occurrence, and seeing their men flying in all directions, being inexperienced and untrained in war, at length found a place of safety from their flight in a certain secluded spot. But in that place the men of Scaldemariland kept being killed with javelins and missiles right up till nightfall. And the night, covering everything with darkness, at last separated the two armies, before the rising of the morning star, the moon the same night shining very slightly. Hereward with 600 men whom he had left the day before to guard the ships, in the dead of night returned to the enemy camp without anyone perceiving it, and there killed many by hurling javelins, as well as wounding a great many, including some officers. It was a complete surprise and as far as the enemy was concerned, beyond all their experience in warfare. When, in full daylight both armies had drawn themselves up in line for the engagement, the men of Scaldemariland hastily sent ambassadors, praying and entreating their opponents for mercy. A bargain was made, the enemy promising that they would do every justice for their wrong-doing, and like slaves would serve their lords, and if they should find favour with them, that they would deliver over to their sway all the men who had laid hands upon their ambassadors, or had consented to it, or who had offended in word or deed, from the least to the greatest. Having received hostages they gladly accepted them, arranging that they would send them an answer on the seventh day.

XIII. Where Hereward got a mare of very great speed, and a colt of conspicuous beauty, and what he underwent on the road.

Meanwhile it was reported to Hereward that there was a remarkable breed of very swift horses in an island of the country. He proceeded thither with a few fellow soldiers and with some who were well acquainted with the difficulties of the route, and got from that place a mare of very great speed, and a colt of conspicuous beauty, which he called Lightfoot and the dam he called Swallow. Now as he was returning from that place, he fell among a band of robbers in a secluded spot among the valleys and hills and woods, where for two days he vigorously withstood their ambushes. On the third day, much weakened by hunger and confused by the violence of the robbers they pressed forward and on the sixth day, having travelled at great speed they arrived at their company's position. Next day they had to make answer to the chiefs of that land, concerning the peace which had transpired and for which they had prayed. It was on Hereward more than all the rest that depended the favourable nature of the reply and the result of the whole arrangement.

Therefore, on the appointed day the men of Scaldemariland presented themselves with all the most important men, with noble gifts, offering their services, and earnestly begging and entreating for a renewal of the ancient treaties and services, more than a confirmation of them as before as in their fathers' time, declaring they would do service under a most secure covenant from this time for ever. This was accepted, and the lords were greatly enriched by presents for the important men of that country, and with the rating of the land and the tribute doubled, the invading army departed and returned to their own land, greatly delighted at the reward of their valour and victory. But neither their lord who had sent them nor his son was there to meet them, but rather a successor of the Kingdom, and they bewailed the death of their most beloved lord and were affected with the deepest grief and sadness. At length they asked the chiefs of the country and their tribunes, if for their great trouble recently undertaken they would give them any benefit on behalf of their deceased lord, since they had brought back the subjection of the land to which they had been sent and could show them hostages and gifts, and they were paying a double tribute from the land as the price of their labour. Besides, they said, they ought to be remunerated by them for the labour they had had. When at last they realised that there would be no recompensation, then, at Hereward's suggestion the soldiers shared among themselves everything they had brought from Scaldemariland, the act of which caused ill-feeling between Hereward and the son of his late lord.

XIV. How Hereward returned to his country and to his father's house, where he discovered that his brother had been slain the day before; and of the grand vengeance he took the same night.

Hereward spent a few idle days in those places thinking that such attitudes were disgraceful. Then he went away and set out for England with a strong desire to visit his father's and his country which by then was subject to the rule of foreigners and almost ruined by the exactions of many. If in any place, any of his friends or neighbours were still alive, he felt he would like to help them. Hereward took with him as his sole companion Martin, surnamed Lightfoot, and left his two nephews, Siward the White and Siward the Red with the wife he had lately taken.

One evening Hereward arrived at his father's mansion, called Bourne and was hospitably entertained by a certain Pirus, a soldier in the employ of his father, named Asered. Hereward met him in the suburbs of the same town. This man, with his family and neighbours were very sorrowful and full of grief, greatly fearing they were delivered over to the rule of foreigners. What was more grievous to them than all else, they bewailed that they would be in subjection to the men who only the day before had slain the innocent young son of their lord, and spoke of those who were the authors of his death and the reason for it.

They answered Hereward: "To some extent it is a help and comfort in sadness to disclose our grief - but not to involve you, a noble man as we see in our misfortunes, with whom rather we ought to make merry for hospitality's sake. Yet since you seem in everything a famous and noble man, we regard you as some remedy to our sorrow, and therefore we gladly explain the whole matter to you. There was with us a certain youthful son of our lord's, whom his father at his death had commended to his people, with his widowed mother; and he would be his heir, if his brother, Hereward, a man most vigorous and conspicuous in every kind of valour, should not return, whom while still a lad his father had driven from his face for his misdoings. And now three days ago, some men with the consent of the King attacked his inheritance and took it for themselves, killing our very light, the son and heir of our lord while he was protecting his widowed mother against them, as they demanded from her his father's riches and treasures, as well as because he slew those two who had handled her discourteously.

"They cut off his head and set it up over the gate of the house, by way of revenge, because he had killed two Frenchmen - and there it still remains. Alas! wretched men that we are, in that we have no means of vengeance! Would that his brother, now, as we have often heard, a very great man, were here. For then, of a truth, everyone of those men, before the moon set and the sun brought forth the rays of its light, would be lying dead like that son of our lord's."

Hereward hearing these words and sighing to himself, groaned deeply. At length after their conversation, all being sleepy went to bed and Hereward, after lying a little while on his bed, heard in the distance the voices of persons singing, and the sound of the harp and viol, and the merriment of people applauding. Summoning a boy, Hereward asked him what the sound was that he could hear. The boy told him that it was the merriment of persons applauding at the banquet on the occasion of the taking the inheritance of their lord's son, whom they had killed.

After a little while Hereward called his servant and put on his tunic, and took a breastplate and helmet from beneath a black cloth under the cloak of a maid-servant, together with a sword. His servant put on light armour and both men proceeded to the scene of merriment, the guests now overcome with drunkenness, designing to pledge them, for his brother's death, in a draught of a spear-shaft and in wine of sorrow. As Hereward approached he found his brother's head over the gate. Taking it down, he kissed it and wrapped it up in a cloth. Then he advanced behind the door of the building to search for the guests and there by the fireside he saw them all overcome with intoxication and the soldiers reclining in women's laps. There was a jester present singing to a lute, abusing the nation of the English and in the middle of the room the man performed ungainly antics, meant in imitation of English dancing. At last the jester demanded his fee from the chief man, something belonging to the parents of the famous youth recently slain. One of the girls at the banquet not regarding his words, answered: "There is still surviving a famous soldier, brother of the slain youth, whose name is Hereward and well known in our country, who is in Flanders. If he were here, not one of these things would be left here by daybreak."

Indignant at these words the lord of the house retorted: "I know the man, and a thorough scoundrel he is. He stole the gifts which were sent to the prince of our country from Scaldemariland and distributed them unfairly, when he had been by him appointed master of the soldiers. He would have suffered death upon a gibbet, if he had not provided for his safety by flight, not venturing to dwell in any land this side of the Alps". On hearing this the jester abused the name of Hereward as he sang, but Hereward could endure this no longer. He leapt upon him and slew him with a single stroke of his sword. Then he attacked the guests and laid low fourteen of them and their lord, some being through drink unable to rise and others being unable to go to their help as they were unarmed; this took place with the assistance of a single servant whom Hereward had set at the door of the hall, so that whoever escaped his hand, might fall into the hand of the servant. That same night the heads of the dead were fixed over the gate where that of Hereward's brother had been placed, and he gave thanks that his brother's blood was now avenged.

XV. The reason that some fled in alarm from Hereward, and where he chose for himself men of war.

In the morning the men of the district and the neighbours were filled with astonishment at what was done. Almost all the French in that area, greatly alarmed, abandoned the lands that had been assigned to them and fled, lest something similar should happen to them at the hands of such a man, if he should become their neighbour. However, the inhabitants of that area having heard about Hereward flocked to him and congratulated him upon his return to his country and to his paternal inheritance and advised him to guard it with caution, dreading the King's anger when he was familiarised with the events. Hereward, not unmindful of these things gathered together in that place 49 of the bravest men from his paternal inheritance and from his Kinsfolk, equipped with all the requirements of military armour. While these preparations proceeded Hereward took vengeance on some of his enemies in the neighbourhood, who still remained at their own abodes.

XVI. The reason he wished to be made Knight in the English manner, and where he was made Knight.

When Hereward had established himself as leader and lord of such men, and witnessed his band increasing every day by fugitives, and condemned men as well as those that had been disinherited, he called to mind that he had never been, according to the English custom, girt with a sword and belt of a Knight. So, with two of his most eminent men, one named Wynter and the other Gaenoch, he went to the Abbot of Burgh (Peterborough), whose name was Brant, a man of very noble birth, that he might gird him with the sword and belt of a Knight after the English practice, lest, after becoming the chief and leader of many men, the inhabitants of the country should find fault with him for not being a Knight.

On the Feast of the Nativity of the Apostles Peter and Paul he obtained the honour of Knighthood at the hands of the Abbot, and for his honour a monk of Ely, Wilton by name, who was also warden (?) and a friend of Hereward's father, and faithful as a brother, made his companions Knights. Thus he wanted himself and his men to be made Knights, as he had heard it had been ruled by the Frenchmen that if anyone were made Knight by a monk or clerk or by any ordained minister, he ought not to be reckoned among true Knights, but as a false Knight and born out of due time.

Hereward in opposition to this rule, desired nearly all the men that served him and were under his rule to be made Knights by the monks, so that if anyone would serve him he should receive the sword as Knightly custom demands at least from a monk, if from no other. He had often said :"If any man received the Knightly sword from a servant of God and a Knight of the Kingdom of heaven, I know that such a servant displays his valour in every sort of military service, as I have often found by experience." Hence arose the custom among the monks of Ely, that if any man there would be made a Knight, he ought always on the same day to offer his naked sword upon the altar at high mass, and receive it again from the monk that was singing the mass, after the gospel, the sword being put on his bare neck with benediction, and in that way be delivering the sword to the recruit, he was made full Knight. This was the practice of Abbots in those times. Afterwards he entered the Isle of Ely and defended it with its inhabitants against King William, who then had subjected almost all the land. Hereward's different achievements we shall recount and describe in their place.

XVII. How Hereward was sought out by a certain man who desired to kill him, and how the Knight slew him.

Returning to his own people Hereward heard that a certain Frederic had been extensively enquiring of him in many places (he was the brother of the old Earl William de Warenne), that he might seize him and take him in person into the King's presence, to hand him over for punishment; or else that he might cut off his head and set it up in the most public thoroughfare for a sign, as Hereward had exhibited over the gate of his house the heads of those men who had taken his inheritance and slain his brother. And further that he might drive into exile or maim all who still were on Hereward's side, or brought him any assistance. But Hereward with his men at once set about anticipating him, designing to treat him in the same way if by chance they could meet with him .Hereward had heard that he was in Norfolk with a band of soldiers, so that when anything was heard of Hereward he might make his way to the spot with a considerable force of men. But what Frederic had intended for Hereward happened to himself one evening. While he was plotting for the death of Hereward, the latter fell upon him and killed him.

XVIII. Why Hereward departed again to Flanders, where he soon performed some noteworthy deeds.

After this he went into Flanders to his wife whom he had lately taken, promising those whom he had left in England that he would return within a year. Meeting with his wife and the two nephews whom he had left with her at St. Omers, he had scarcely been there a fortnight before he was invited by Baldwin, a very renowned Knight of that province to a contest which he had undertaken against the Viscount of Pynkenni. The lord of Brabant and his nobles were present at this meeting. On this expedition Hereward with his two nephews, Siward the White and Siward the Red with the noble Knight Baldwin who had taken them there, behaved in such a way that even the opposing party could not withhold their commendation, but greatly praised them, especially selecting Hereward for their admiration. On one occasion, advancing too far into the enemy's lines, Hereward was unhorsed and surrounded, himself standing alone.

His enemies gained nothing from the circumstances, but rather they met with speedy destruction, for he slew seven of those who attempted to seize him. At length being surrounded by enemies on all sides, he was helped by some of the principal men of the opposite party that admired his valour and courage, and they drove off his pursuers, saying it was an unworthy act for a great number of men the whole day long to be attacking a single man, and with difficulty prevail at last. Besides, if he were overcome what credit would it be to them if one were overcome by many? Certainly a slur would be placed upon their reputation, and he, though he may fall in the end, would deservedly be esteemed above all.

While Hereward was recovering from the attack and was without a sword, fearful that he might still be seized, a comrade came to his help and caught him up. Mounted on horseback Hereward related to everybody what had happened to him, and recounted with what generosity his enemies had behaved, though he had slain seven of their men who had incautiously attacked him. This produced such good feeling in both parties that all who were formerly at variance, out of respect for such grand a Knight, made peace, and he was honoured and loaded with gifts.

XIX. How on Hereward's return to England his men gathered themselves together on his giving the signal arranged at his departure.

As he had promised, Hereward returned to England with his two nephews now eminent in all military knowledge and with his wife Turfrida who went far beyond the common weakness of women, proving capable in every emergency that occurred to her famous husband. With him there came a Chaplain, Hugo Britannious by name, who although a priest was not less endued with the skill and knowledge of arms. There were others Wirhardus his brother, a Knight of great repute in valour, bringing with him some men that were in his service. Some of these Hereward sent at once to explore his own district and his father's house, to make diligent enquiry as to what had been settled between him and the King. He also ascertained with the greatest caution from his friends around his native place where those men were whom he had left in England. When those whom Hereward had despatched arrived at the place of his boyhood they found his inheritance quite unmolested, no men daring to enter it. Some of his old comrades they found in hiding and they were provided for their own safety. These men, delighted at his return, hastened to join him, namely one Wynter, a famous Knight short in stature but excessively robust and strong and Wenotus and Alutus Gurgan, notable in all valour and bravery for being tall and big they were very efficient. With them were three more nephews of Hereward, Godwin Gille, so-called because not unlike Godwin the son of Guthlac who is celebrated in stories of the ancients; and Duti and Outi, twin brothers, alike in character and in person and of repute as soldiers. But the rest of the band of followers were scattered over the whole Kingdom. Hereward had devised a signal at his departure which he would use to recall them; accordingly he set fire to three villages over Bruneswold near Bourne and then departed into the woods until his men had gathered together.

When they were all assembled all were most eminent men - not one of them to be esteemed worthy of Knightly dignity unless he had first achieved some memorable deeds. These are their names, making (with those we have named above) the whole number: Wluncus The Black, so-called because he had stained his face with charcoal and gone unrecognised among some enemies who were in security and had overthrown ten of them with his single spear. His mate was Wluricas Rahere, or The Heron, so-called because he was by chance at Wrokesham Bridge where four innocent brothers were condemned to be executed and terrifying the executioners who called him a Heron in mockery, he manfully caused the innocent men to be liberated and some of their enemies killed. Others too were associated with the more famous of Hereward's Knights, Godricus of Corby, nephew of the Earl of Warwick, and Tosti of Davenesse, kinsman of the same Earl, whose name he acquired in baptism, and Acere Vasus, son of a gentleman near Lincoln who owned the tower of the city (?), and Lewinus Mone, that is The Sickle, so-called because being by chance in a meadow when he was cutting the grass by himself, he was set upon by a score of labourers of the place with pitchforks and spears in their hands, and alone among them all, with nothing but his sickle he wounded many and killed some, dashing among them like a reaper and so put them all to flight.

In company with those already mentioned was also one named Turbentinus, greatgrandson of Earl Edwin and Lefwinus Prat, that is The Crafty, because though often captured by his enemies he had cunningly escaped, many times killing his guards. With them were others most experienced in warfare: Leofric the Deacon, and Villicus of Drayton (perhaps an officer, bailiff - not a name), and Turkillys and Utlamhe, that is The Outlaw, Hereward's cook Hogor, his kinsman Winter and Liveret, two men of mark, and Radenaldus, steward of Ramsey; these were standard bearers. So too were Wluricus The Black and Wluricus The White, Wluricas Grugam, Ylardus, Godwinus Gille, Outi, with those named before, and those two spendid men - Siward The White and Siward The Red, Hereward's nephews. There were also other very famous Knights, Godricus of Corby, Hugo the Norman, a priest, and Ylardus his brother, Leofric the Deacon, Tosti of Rothwell and Godwinus of Rothwell, Osbernus, Alsinus, Lefwinus Prat, Hurchillus and Villicus of Drayton. All of these were the most renowned and splendid Knights in the Kingdom and there were several others whom it would be tedious to enumerate individually.

XX. How the men in the Isle of Ely sent for Hereward and how on the road he discovered an ambush of the Earl of Warenne.

Now the men in the Isle of Ely had begun to hold the island against King William who had won England in war. Hearing the return of Hereward they sent for him desiring him to come with all his men and take part with them in the defence of their country and the liberty of their fathers, assuring him that he would in every way be most highly esteemed among them. These messages were delivered to Hereward more especially in the name and on behalf of Thurstan, Abbot of the Church of Ely and his monks, the Isle of Ely being their dominion and it were they who had put it in a state of defence against the King, more particularly because he had designed to set a certain foreign monk over them; one of those monks for whom he had already sent from the French nation, to appoint as deans and heads in all the English churches.

However, a famous soldier, Brumannus by name, well acquainted with the coast and having knowledge of this, met the French priests at sea, dipped them all in the sea in a large sack that he had attached to the prow of his vessel, and sent them back. Thus for a time he delivered the monasteries of the English and their friends from foreign rule. Hereward was delighted with the Ely mens invitation and at once set out on the journey, embarking at Bardney (near Lincoln). Hearing this the Earl of Warenne, whose brother Hereward had lately slain, prepared several ambushes by the road in secret places near the marsh, and with caution placed guards round the waters by the side of the land hoping to take Hereward without serious loss of his own men. These schemes were made known to Hereward some of the guards having set foul of a number of stragglers of Hereward's force. Hereward despatched men to help them and captured the attacking party, and from them he ascertained that the ambush was formed by the Earl of Warenne and that he himself was coming to Herbeche the next day. Hereward made haste and stationed his ships and men at the spot and hid some armed men near the river bank. Then he himself with three Knights and four archers all well armed, went close to the river bank where the Earl and his men had just arrived on the opposite site.

On seeing them one of the Earl's men drew near and said: "Are you of the company of that scoundrel Hereward who has by cunning ruined such numbers and has drawn so many to himself to help his nefarious deeds? I wish the rascal could be betrayed to our lord the Earl: if you will conive at this he will deem you worthy of reward and honour. For this force of the enemy - though not dangerous - may drive us to this, to dwell in a dismal swamp and to pursue one without arms through a muddy marsh and among the eddies of the waters and the sharp reeds, everyone of them destined to death together with the leader at an early date. By now the King has entirely surrounded the Isle of Ely with his army and has closed in the whole land, that he may destroy all its inhabitants." At these words one of Hereward's men replied: "How much longer you wretch will you try to persuade us to betray and desert our master? Make haste and withdraw lest you fall beneath our fierce javelins; and tell your lord that the man for whom he is asking is on this side of the water."

At this intelligence the Earl immediately presented himself and on seeing Hereward urged all his men to swim across the water with him, to avenge his brothers death. But his men declared that they could not do that, saying that Hereward had come there for the very purpose of beguiling them in that manner, whereupon the Earl, with a groan addressed the men across the water: "Oh! if that man of Belial, your master, were now in my hands. He should of a truth taste his due punishment, death." Hearing these words Hereward replied: "Yes! and if by good fortune we were both by ourselves in any place, you would not obtain your wish that I should be in your weak hands, nor would you have reason to be glad of our meeting." Then, Hereward, leaning forward a little, stretched his bow and discharged an arrow with great force upon the breast of the Earl. Although it glided off the corselet that protected him, yet he was almost killed by the blow. At this, his men very anxious for their lord who had fallen off his horse at the blow, quickly carried him away in their arms.

Hereward went away and on the same day arrived with his men in the Isle of Ely where he was received with the greatest respect by the Abbot and the monks. He was much honoured by the principal men of the place, namely by Adwin, Earl of Leicester and his brother Morkere, Earl of Warwick, and another Earl, Tosti by name who had all fled to the men of the Isle. They had suffered many wrongs at the hands of King William, being worried with many grievous exactions, and like other eminent men of the country had gone to the Isle.

XXI. How the King attempted to take the Isle and nearly lost his entire army, and no man except one brave knight, entered it.

When the King heard of these things he was excessively angry. Impelled by great indignation he urgently attempted to take the Isle. First he moved all his army to Alrehede where it was not so wholly surrounded with waters and swamp; the breadth of this position extended only four furlongs. After bringing instruments and engines of logs and stones and piles of all sorts, they constructed a causeway in the swamp, though it was comparatively useless and narrow, near to the great river by the place, namely Alrehede. They also put in the water very large trees and beams bound together, and beneath them sheep-skins tied together, turned after flaying and inflated with air, so that the weight of men going over it might be better borne.

When this was done, a great multitude of men rushed upon it, eager among other things to get to the gold and silver which was thought to be plentifully hidden in the Isle, with the result that those men who, in their haste, had taken the lead were drowned and the causeway that they had made collapsed into the marsh with them. Those that were in the middle of the company were also swallowed up in the watery and deep swamp. A few indeed of those who followed last with the loss of their arms, escaped with difficulty, tumbling out of the water through the sand. Although hardly a man pursued them, they perished in great numbers in the waters and in the swamp; and of those that perished, up to this very day, are drawn from the depths of those waters, in rotten armour. This we have sometimes ourselves seen.

Of all those mentioned above not one got into the Isle, except by mere chance a single eminent Knight called Dada, who was at the very front. No man defending the Isle was caught in the snare, for some men had made a heap of sods on the bank of the river in front of the bulwarks and ramparts, laying ambushes on the right and on the left. The King observing all these things from a distance, saw how his men in front were swallowed up in the swamp and waters. Groaning from heartfelt sorrow with those of his men who still survived - very few compared with the number that were drowned the King departed, laying aside all hope of making any further attack on the Isle. However, he put a guard there, and soldiers round about, lest the Saxon islanders should have free access to lay waste the district.

XXII. Of a soldier who went into the Isle and resolved to be the first to give information to the King about the Isle and its inhabitants.

That Norman soldier whom we have named previously as having gone into the Isle, was taken prisoner and led before the chief men and dignitaries of the Isle of Ely. When he was asked the reason of his coming and his name, it was discovered that he was called Dada, and the reason of his coming was as follows: The King, in the presence of his followers, had made a bargain that whoever should first make his way into the Isle and inflict some damage, might ask of him any of the possessions in the Isle; furthermore the King promised that he should have it. Hearing this the Isle defenders praised the enemy soldier's audacity and valour, and they caused him to stay with them for a few days that he might become acquainted with their valour, and see how secure a position they held, being provided with the defence of a thoroughly fortified place and in no small degree strengthened by companies of distinguished soldiers. For, as he frequently declared in their presence, he had many times heard that they were less proficient in war and less skilled in military tactics than other nations.

Before Dada left the Isle of Ely he perceived that they were most excellent in every way and efficient in the practice of warfare. He was allowed to leave on these terms: that he should report about them nothing more than what he had heard and seen, and this he had to confirm with an oath. At length, complimented with a present, he arrived at the King's court and everybody congratulated him on his arrival and the King himself was glad, for Dada was a man of very great repute among the more distinguished of the King's Knights. When he was asked before the whole court, he declared how he entered the Isle by some favour of fortune safe and sound. While on the causeway on which they had made and had marched, great numbers, as we have narrated above, had perished, he said that he alone of them all had been conducted alive by Hereward the master of the soldiers of the Isle into that place. By him, Dada asserted he had been honoured among the most distinguished of the bands of soldiers. Afterwards, on enquiry, Hereward learned the reason of his going there, Dada explaining to him the King's promise that any man who should first go into the Isle and inflict some damage should be rewarded with very great honour. Upon being further strictly questioned, he went through all the dignitaries of the chief men of the Isle and their names, and recounted the grandeur of their defensive works and how well strengthened they were by troops of distinguished soldiers and in no small degree protected by companies of mighty men.

In the first place of order he put those three Earls already named, that is to say, Adwinus, Morkere and Tosti, and the two nobles Orgar and Thrachitell, surnamed, The Boy. In giving his description of them he extolled Hereward the Outlaw with his men above themselves and above all Knights whom he had ever seen in France, or in the Roman Empire, or in Constantinople, for their valour and courage, and if he thought some equal to him (Hereward) yet, said Dada, no one could surpass him. At this the Earl of Warenne, whose brother we have already said Hereward had lately slain, moved with anger and stirred up with great indignation, spoke out: "Truly it is very evident that you are wholly deceived in that you would untruthfully induce our lord the King to show kindness by extolling his enemies with false and specious praises. And above all do you set up that most infamous man Hereward for valour and courage? Let his Majesty be no more burdened with such frivolous talk." To whom Dada made reply: He had not been seduced by bribe or present, nor was any favour promised in the future, except that he was to tell the truth about them without fear or favour, and he was allowed freely to depart after having taken an oath to do this. He then proceeded to enquire how he could keep silence on these matters while he was asked what he himself had seen and experienced, without offending his lord the King and violating his oath if he gave untruthfully any other report.

The King commanded that Dada was to be regarded as harmless for those matters and that he should tell them more, professing that he had long known him for a truth telling soldier, and he believed he was not exaggerating now. Once more Dada was thoroughly questioned not only by the King but also by many others. His questioners asked if the enemy were in need of provisions or any necessaries, or if there were any more famous men in addition to those he had previously named, so as to find out if he would contradict himself in his account; or rather that they might discover something to help them in their attack. To all this Dada had but one answer: "If you are still anxious to learn the reason (of their enmity), it is as follows, as I have often heard. His Majesty had arranged that monks from across the sea ought to be appointed as deans and heads in all the English churches; and your Majesty had lately sent for them. These men, a famous English Soldier, Brumannus by name, intercepted while at sea for that reason, and dipped them in the sea in a large sack and made them go back. By this action he delivered his friends for a time from foreign rule. For which cause the monks of that place (Ely), fearing to be subjected to foreigners preferred rather to work than to be reduced to slavery. They, therefore, gathered to themselves the outlaws, the condemned, the disinherited, and their parents, and fortified their territory and the Isle against them and others to some slight extent."

"Within the Isle there is no pressure by reason of the number of their army and no enemy pressed them, seeing that though blockaded by four Kings and their people, nothing seems to affect their daily life; the ploughman does not take his hand from the plough, nor does the reaper's right hand waver in the harvest, nor does the hunter neglect his hunting spears, nor does the fowler cease from lying in wait for birds by the banks of rivers, and in the woods. The inhabitants are well and plentifully supplied with all sorts of living creatures. For at the time when the water fowl change their feathers and appearance, there I have often seen men bring many little birds, sometimes a hundred, occasionally two hundred and more, and very often not many less than a thousand from one single piece of water. And from the woods that are in the Isle of Ely, in the same way, at one time of the year there is a great supply of herons, to say nothing of the abundance of wild animals and cattle. Then again from the waters round the Isle, it is very well known that they abound with every kind of fish. Why need I say more? For every day that I spent my time there in the English manner we felt disgust at the banquets in the monks' refectory, soldier and monk repairing together to dinner and supper. At the high table sat the Abbot with the three Earls already named, and the two distinguished men Hereward and Turkillus surnamed Pure, seated side by side.

"Above each Knight and monk shields and lances hung against the wall, and in the middle of the hall from one end to the other were breastplates and helmets and other pieces of armour, so that always the monks as well as the soldiers were quite ready to take their turn and go forth on a warlike expedition. In truth this one thing above all others struck me as marvellous: of the things I noticed, the monks of that place are so well versed in warfare, something that I never heard of before, nor have I experienced such a thing in any other place. For I do not know that they are deficient in anything pertaining to their defence, unless perhaps in personal courage, while they have a fertile Isle, most productive in every kind of seed and grain, and so well protected by waters and swamp - much stronger than any castle surrounded by walls. Yet I trust my lord the King will not cease from attacking them, and he will find my account quite truthful and he will discover that he had better make peace with them than be continually attacking them and getting nowhere."

XXIII. What the Normans did when they were disheartened about the Isle, and how the King was disposed to make peace with them but was dissuaded by some of his own men.

While Dada was relating this a soldier whom the King had appointed to construct the blockade and the dyke at Reach, waited for the speaker to finish, then said: "Are these things incredible to you and do they seem false? Only yesterday I saw some men coming from the Isle, not a great number - no more than seven - in the dress of soldiers and armed with proper equipment for war, all of whom were doubtlessly monks except two. They were well acquainted with warfare like the rest of the soldiers and claimed to exercise the rights of a soldier. They set fire to Burwell and inflicted mischief into every direction, and not only they, but others also, running about. Some of our men, ten in number, working in front of us, on the blockade, hurried without consideration to themselves, hoping to capture them as they were of a smaller number than ourselves, at length came up with them by the dyke, within distance of throwing lances. After a great deal of fighting our men at last succumbed, but one managed to survive - a fine soldier, Richard by name and by surname Grandson of the Viscount Osbertus, to whom, apart from the main body a man named Wenochus had stuck closely in an attempt to take him.

"While these were long fighting and the Isle men were awaiting and could see neither prevailing, they observed us with a band of soldiers drawing near. Their leader, Hereward, caused them to separate and forbad anyone to offer violence to Richard, saying it was unworthy for two or three to fight against one and that he would on no account allow such a thing to be done by his men. This we learned from the mouth of the man himself. Finally, we pursued them to their ships and we killed one of their sailors with a javelin and caught another. And he recounted to us their dignitaries and who they were, adding their names: Hereward the leader of the soldiers, Wenochus, Turstanaus, a young man who was afterwards surnamed Warden, Boter of Saint Edmunds, Siwardus, Levricus, and Acer the Hard, so-called because he was hardy in enduring labour". Although these men were monks, they were most distinguished in all military knowledge and often, with Hereward, made trial of valourous deeds, being thoroughly approved in their training. But the King said nothing not a word either good or bad - thinking to himself that it was an unworthy thing to abuse men who acted valiantly and yet unwilling to extol his enemies before his own men. He contemplated making peace with them, for he was aware that the Isle of Ely was protected both by nature and by very brave men; he perceived that he could in no way prevent their going in and out.

Summoning the nobles and councillors, the King explained to them what was in his mind, that it was his wish to make peace with the Isle men, declaring it was too serious a thing to leave such men in the middle of the land in his rear, when they ought to be marching against the Danish army, and after that to go directly to Normandy. At that, some of the elders present and closest to him, at once began to dissuade the King from his purpose, because the men of the Isle had invaded many of their estates, and had taken shares of their possessions. The elders said: "If you dismiss without punishment those who have long and vigorously been raging against your rule and agree to make peace with them without their begging for it humbly and with prayers, and when rights are granted to them, all men will mock at your superiority and none will be afraid to act likewise in your dominion." The King replied with anger, saying that he could not take the Isle of Ely, nor any place so fortified naturally by the power of God. To this, one present, Ivo Taillebois by name, indignantly answered :"I have known for a long time an old woman who could if she were here, by her single skill, crush all their valour and all their defences, and drive them all in alarm away from the Isle." On hearing this all present at once began to persuade the King to give consent, saying that they ought not to oppose but rather to assist, and enrich with very great presents, anyone who could by skill or ability or in any way whatever, crush the enemies of the King's Majesty. The King yielded to their persuasions and immediately ordered the old woman to be brought to him in secret and that it was not to be done openly. Afterwards, he gathered his army and surrounded the Isle, guarding it everywhere, himself appointing sentinels here and there, and ordering a blockade, lest anyone should come out from the Isle and discover what was being planned towards taking it, whereby they might contrive some art or invention against them.

XXIV. How Hereward dressed up as a potter and went to the King's court to discover what they intended doing; and how he cheated them and slew some in the King's court and returned unharmed.

The King having arranged these things, the Isle was so effectively guarded from the outside that almost all means of entrance and exit was stopped. This was a cause for grief and alarm among the Isle's inhabitants, since they did not know what the King's men intended to do against them, nor what plan of attack was being formed, since they had heard that the King had knowledge of some new fashion of making war. They therefore decided that they ought somehow or other to send a man outside the Isle to explore. But finding no one quite fit for the purpose, it seemed good to Hereward that he himself go out in disguise, a suggestion strongly objected to by all. At last Hereward set out, taking with him his mare called Swallow, a creature always lean and ugly in appearance, whose speed we have already commented on, and how ready she was to undergo fatigue. As he went out he changed his attire, cut his hair and beard and put on a dirty coat. Meeting a potter, he took his pots and assuming the character of a potter made his way to the King's court at Brandon. Arriving there the same night as it happened, Hereward spent the night at the house of a widow where that witch, already mentioned, dwelt - the witch who was fetched to destroy the men of the Isle. There, at night, Hereward heard the women talking to each other in the Roman language, how they were to contrive to vanquish the Isle, for they regarded him as a rustic unacquainted with the language.

In the middle of the night Hereward saw them go out quietly to a spring of water that flowed towards the east near the garden of the house. He followed them immediately and at a distance heard them conversing, questioning and getting replies from some unknown guardian of the spring. Hereward designed to cut them off as they returned, but their lengthy stay prevented this and as it happened left him to undertake more magnificent deeds of daring. Next morning Hereward took up his pots and departed. He roamed all around the King's court and kept crying out in potter's fashion, in English, "Pots! pots! Good pots and jars! First class earthenware!" Meanwhile he was taken by some servants into the King's kitchen, so that they might buy some pots. One of the overseers of the town, coming by chance, on seeing Hereward, cried out at once that he had never seen a man so like Hereward in the face, nor so like him in bearing, as far as a poor man could resemble a gentleman, or a country labourer a soldier.

Some men hearing this came to look at the man so like Hereward, and he was taken into the King's hall among the soldiers and recruits, for them to see. Looking intently at him some said that a man of such moderate height could not possess so much valour and courage as common report assigned to Hereward, and others asked him if he knew or had ever seen that scoundrel. To whom he answered: "I wish that man of Belial were now here among us, a man hated by me more than anybody, for now I would wreak my vengeance on him. For he carried off a cow of mine and four sheep and everthing I had except my pots and beast, whereby hitherto I have supported myself and my two sons." By now the King's dinner was to be got ready and Hereward went back to the kitchen. After dinner the servants and cooks and the kitchen boys with them offered him wine and strong drink to make him drunk, and made great fun of him. At last mellowed with wine, they wanted to shave his head and pull out the hairs of his beard, and to blindfold him and so make him break his own pots which they put all about the ground for this purpose. As Hereward was disinclined to submit to their jests one man drew near and gave him a severe blow. Hereward returned the blow under the ear to such effect that the man fell to the ground as if dead. Seeing this his companions rose against Hereward with three-pronged forks and pitchforks, so he seized a brand from a hearth and defended himself against them all, killing one man and wounding many more. This was immediately made known in the palace and he was apprehended and delivered into custody. While in custody, the King having just gone out with a hunting party, one of the Keepers came up carrying fetters in one hand with which he threatened to place on Hereward; in the other hand he held an unsheathed sword. At once Hereward seized him, and fell upon him with the man's own sword, so that he tasted death, and after that Hereward killed several others.

Being thus set free, Hereward went over hedges and ditches to the upper court of the house where he found his horse. As he was mounting, one of the King's boys saw him and upbraided him with bad language, giving warning to his companions to pursue him at once

29

with the King's servants, declaring that he had escaped out of chains. Hereward could not tolerate his scolding words, and when the boy put himself in his way struck him through with his sword. Whereupon many pursued him, but the pursuers were too slow and Hereward too fast, and passing through the island of Somersham all through the evening and night by moonlight, at early dawn Hereward arrived in due course at the Isle. Of all those who pursued him no-one had heard a single word of him or seen any traces, except one who by chance had proceeded further up the wood and suddenly his horse broke down from fatigue and the man himself could scarcely stand up on his feet. Hereward, coming upon him accidentally found him lying on the ground nearly breathless. He asked him who he was, and the man replied: "One of the attendants of the King's courtiers who have been following a country fellow that has escaped, by whom this day one of the King's boys and the custodians of the fellow have guilefully been slain. If you have heard or seen anything, for God's sake, and of your great kindness tell me."

"Now," said Hereward, "since you ask for God's sake and of my great kindness, know that I am myself the man you are seeking. And that you may know me better and may be able to declare most truthfully to the lord your King that you have spoken with me, you shall leave behind your sword and lance for a token and you shall give me your promise that you will render him a true account, if you wish to save your life." At length the servant got back and as he had promised told the King, while all men listened with amazement, about Hereward; and the King protested that he was a man of noble soul and a most distinguished warrior.

XXV. How Hereward disguised himself as a fisherman and cheated the King a second time: and how the King attacked the Isle and about the islanders' means of defence.

The King, as he arranged, in pursuit of the object for which he had directed his march to the spot - when the engines of war were made ready, attempted to carry out his plans, leading his whole army to Alreheche. He also arranged for a large pile of wood and stones and a heap of all kinds of timber to be brought thither. The King then commanded all the fishermen of the province to come with their boats to Cotingelade, so that they might transport what they had brought to the place and with the materials construct mounds and hillocks on the top of which they might fight. Among these Hereward came with the rest like a fisherman with a boat and they carefully transported everything that they had brought there. At last on the same day, the sun not setting without some damage done before he departed, Hereward finished his work and set it on fire, whereby the whole was burnt up and some men were killed by it and some drowned.

Hereward had gone with his head and beard shaven so as not to be recognised, employing different disguises for the death and destruction of his foes, more willing to appear for a time in ungainly fashion and to lose his comely hair than to spare his adversaries. When this was reported that Hereward had with impunity again got away, the King said it had been a shameful thing that on more than one occasion he had been mocked by the man. Yet the worthy King among other things and above all, ordered his men and charged them that Hereward should be brought to him alive, and they should keep him unharmed. Being much impressed with the damage done on this occasion, the King's men set guards over all their property and over the works, night and day. So for seven days they struggled and with much difficulty completed one work. They set up four circular timber erections on which to place the engines, but the Isle men, erecting outworks and bulwarks to oppose them, made a vigorous resistance. On the eighth day, all advanced to attack the Isle of Ely with their whole strength and they put that witch previously mentioned on an elevated spot among them, so that she being sufficiently protected on all sides, might have free room for the exercise of her skill.

When she had got up she spoke out for a long time against the Isle and its inhabitants, denouncing destruction and uttering charms for their overthrow and at the end of her talking and incantations the witch turned her back upon them in derision. After she had gone through this disgusting ceremony three times as she had proposed, behold, the men who were hidden all around in the swamp, on the right and left, among the reeds and rough briars of the swamp set the reeds on fire and by the help of the wind the smoke and flames spread in the direction of and up to the Norman camp. Extending some two furlongs the fire rushing hither and thither among them formed a horrible spectacle in the marsh, and the roar of the flames with the crackling twigs of brushwood and willows made a terrible noise. Stupified and very alarmed, the Normans fled, each man for himself; but they could not go far through the desert parts of the swamp in that watery road, and they found great difficulty keeping to the path. Very many were suddenly swallowed up and others drowned in the same waters and overwhelmed with arrows, for in the fire their javelins were no good against the groups of men who came out cautiously and secretly from the Isle to repel them. Among them that woman of infamous art, hysterical with fear, fell down head first from her lofty frame and broke her neck.

The great King himself among the few (compared to the number of those that died) who had managed to escape, carried in his shield as he made his way to the camp at the rear, an arrow that had struck deep. On seeing this his men were alarmed supposing him to be wounded, and they loudly bewailed the accident. To quieten them, the King said: "I have no wound to complain of, but I do complain that I did not take a sound design from all those that were submitted to me - and that is why nearly all our men have fallen, deceived by the subtlety of an infamous woman and moved without knowledge of her detestable art, even to listen to whom ought to have been for us an accursed thing, for so these things would not have happened to us."

At this time Earl Radulfus, surnamed Waer, having secretly gathered together a very large army, had invited certain people of the English nation to his wedding, and had compelled them by force and trickery to bind themselves to him by oath, and he laid waste and subjugated to himself the whole land from Norwich to Tedford and Sudbury. The three Earls and elders who were in the Isle of Ely, had gone off with him as though he meant to make a claim for the Kingdom and country, leaving Hereward with his men to guard the Isle.

XXVI. How and why the men of Ely made an agreement with the King, whereupon Hereward wanted to burn the church and town.

Notwithstanding all these preparations the King, perceiving that his energy was of no avail to obtain possession of the Isle of Ely by war or by force, and considering the large number of men he had now lost all at once, and the great number lost previously, made a decree to divide amongst his more eminent followers lands of Ely church which lay outside the Isle together with the property of monks. They would therefore only need to guard the Isle from without. Some of the King's men, therefore, appropriating to their own use the lands of the church nearby, claimed them for themselves. The monks of Ely, hearing of this, adopting a more prudent plan in their undertakings upon the return of the Abbot who had gone in disguise to Angerhale with the ornaments and treasure of the church. He had asked the King for conditions of peace, and that he restore to them all the lands of the church freely and honourably. This was done on a certain day in secret, that it might not come to Hereward's knowledge. The messengers were received graciously by the King, and they made arrangements for him to come at once, secretly to the Isle when Hereward should happen to have gone with his men foraging, so that the affair might be managed without bloodshed and grievous slaughter. But one of the monks Alwinus the son or Orgar, went to him to tell him that they (the Abbot and the Monks) had already received the King and made a covenant with him.

He soon met Hereward on the road from the bank with his men, carrying torches to set fire to the church and town in consequence of what he had heard. The monk with many prayers and entreaties opposed the design, urging Hereward to consult his own safety by flight, if unwilling to join them in securing peace, adding also that the King with all his army was near Witchford, within a furlong's distance. Yielding at length to his persuasive words, because he regarded him as a friend and good comrade in warfare and in many of his necessities efficient; also because he was convinced by his arguments, Hereward decided upon immediate action and with his vessels which he had well provided with arms to guard the waters round about the Isle, withdrew to a certain sea called Wide, near Welle, a piece of large water with ample channels and having ready means of egress. There he designed to wait because he had despatched some of his men to Cissahum to inflict mischief and lay the land waste with fire until the scouts that he had sent secretly should quickly lead the men to him to prevent their being captured. The men were found at last in a little island called Stimtencia and they thought that Hereward's scouts were pursuing them and hid themselves at some distance in the marsh among the reeds. Two of them, Starcufulfi and Broker, lurking together, thought it might give them a better chance of safety if they had the tonsure, like monks. So with their swords in the best way they could, they made a tonsure for each other. At last some words shouted out produced mutual recognition, and all in one body retraced their steps to their lord Hereward.

XXVII. How Hereward was reduced to such straits that he slew with his own hands his excellent horse: and how next he overcame the army of five provinces.

After a period of freedom from severe pursuit in the Wide Sea, Hereward was urgently besieged by some men of his own province and of the King's men. He was reduced to such straits that in despair he slew with his own hands his excellent horse, so that no man of lower rank should boast that he had got Hereward's horse. At last he escaped with his men from this peril and passed over into Brunneswald; in like manner he went on to dwell in the great woods of Northamptonshire, laying the land waste with fire and sword. Due to this action the King commanded an army to be gathered from these nine provinces (only seven are named): Northampton, Cambridge, Lincoln, Holland, Leicester, Huntingdon and Warwick, which on an appointed day with a host of soldiers attempted to take Hereward and his men, searching for him all about the woods near Bourne, where at the time he was staying. Surrounded by his enemies, when he had no opportunity of getting away from them, he moved about from place to place in the more remote parts of that district, awaiting the arrival of his men and the friends he had sent to help him. Meanwhile, he caused the shoes on his horse's feet to be reversed, so that it could not be discovered from their tracks where they were going or where they were.

Hereward instructed his friends and fellow soldiers to do the same. His friends had arrived one by one as best as they could, and Hereward had seen that there was no place to turn to, because war was pressing him all around. It seemed good to him to make an attack upon the enemy with a small number of men, either in their rear, or van, or flank, before they could be prepared for fighting, since now there were with him a hundred picked soldiers and two hundred very sturdy men, besides a few slingers and archers. As it happened in those days Hereward had several men both foreigners and natives who had come to him for military training and who, in order to be instructed in warfare, had left their masters and friends and had gone to Hereward on hearing the fame of his men; and some men came even of the King's own courtiers, to find out if what they had heard of him could possibly be true. But Hereward received these with great caution and imposed an oath of fidelity.

For there was a very great multitude of soldiers and foot soldiers of those provinces, and Turoldus, Abbot of Burgh (Peterborough) and Ivo Taillebois were leading the King's army, so as to kill them all. Then Hereward and his men, not alarmed at their numbers, and notwithstanding that they were grievously beset on all sides, got themselves ready and concealed all their archers and slingers among the trees, discharging their weapons from above, and secretly stationed themselves among the trunks of trees, that when fighting below they might be protected by them and so make a defence, lest they should be unable to endure the onset when the violent rush was made upon them. And they advanced from cover of the thicket under the protection of their archers, Hereward in everything always leading the way. Immediately after him came Rahenaldus, steward of Ramsey, who always acted as standardbearer in Hereward's army, and other most renowned soldiers had positions given on the right and left; the names of which most renowned men, and their valour in so famous a contest, in memory of what a few achieved against so many, we think it proper to record. The first then of them and rightly regarded as first in knowledge of warfare and in courage - a man named Winter - was on the left side. These had gone forth on horseback, not inconsiderately to take the lead in the attack. In this enterprise they, becoming separated from the rest, were rushing upon the enemy they broke through the first line and slew many; and having inflicted some damage, returned to the woods for cover, for fear they should be unable to withstand the host of the enemy if they attacked in force. Yet after a while they retraced their steps and returned, and so all day long over and over again they came out and went back again, attacking great numbers of the enemy, their own friends protecting them with weapons hurled from above, and securing their safety when the Normans retreated. The Saxon army strove up to the ninth hour, the horses of their adversaries as well as uniformed soldiers being exceedingly provoked, pursuing them as they fled and waiting in arms all day long for them to come out, until at last they withdrew from blockading the camp. |

Then immediately Hereward with all his men came upon them from the rear in one rush with severe engagement and captured some of the enemy including five men of great importance, keeping them as prisoners. Among these the Abbot of Burgh (Peterborough) was captured as well as others of the greatest renown. The Norman adversaries, seeing this, ceased fighting, although they had got to close quarters, for fear that their enemies should illtreat or even slay those whom they had captured. We have previously described the extraordinary progress of their fighting. This last engagement proved a great blow and no small destruction to the Norman army which was utterly worn out with it and the fatigue, and being at a distance from camp now began to make its way back to it.

XXVIII. How Hereward took vengeance upon the Abbot of Burgh.

After the Abbot of Burgh had been delivered from the hand of Hereward by payment of a substantial ransom, and the nephew of the same abbot and all the others whom they had captured had been dismissed by one of Hereward's kinsmen, Siward the White (whom he had lately treated with great hospitality), out of respect of the Abbot, remembering neither their covenant nor the benefit received, they recompensed Hereward by again making war upon him and his men. To this end the Abbot granted many of the possessions of his church to soldiers on condition they supplied forthwith military assistance to subdue Hereward in respect to the trouble the Abbot experienced through him; and he arranged that they should attack Hereward as service for their lands. Now when Hereward heard these reports and that a penalty was hanging over him for his kindness, without delay the same night they might avenge themselves, he went with his men to Burgh (Peterborough), and laid waste the whole town with fire, plundered all the treasure of the church and overtook the Abbot although he with his men would have escaped by hiding themselves.

XXIX. Of a vision and a marvellous occurence seen by Hereward.

During the following night in his sleep Hereward saw standing by him a man of indescribable form, old, terrible of aspect, in all his clothing more remarkable than anything he had seen or imagined, threatening him with a great key which he carried in his hand, and with a terrible injunction that he should restore in their entirety all those belongings of his church which he had taken on the past night, if he wished to provide for his own safety and escape a miserable death next day. On waking Hereward was seized with holy terror and the same hour took back everything he had taken away, and then with all his men he departed. On their journey they went astray and lost the right road. But a marvellous thing happened to them as they were straying - a miracle, if in truth it can be said that such things can happen to men. In the darkness of the night and during a storm while wandering hither and thither through the woods they knew not where they were going, a huge wolf came in front of them, fawning upon them like a tame dog. Coming nearer on the path the animal walked before them.

Thinking him, in the darkness, to be a white dog, they encouraged one another to follow the animal closely, believing it to have come from some town. This they did and in the silence of the night at a time when they had succeeded in getting out of the byway and recognised their road, quite suddenly there appeared burning flames attached to the soldiers' lances - not very bright - but like those which the common people call Fairies' Lights. Nor could any man get rid of them or put them out or throw them away. Whereupon in great wonder although stupified they proceeded along the right road, guided by the dog. At dawn, to their astonishment they discovered at last that a wolf had been their guide. While they marvelled at what had happened to them, the wolf disappeared and the flames went out, and they came to the place they had intended, beyond Stamford. Seeing that the journey had been prosperously accomplished they gave thanks to God, grateful for what had happened to them.

XXX.

After a stay of almost three days Hereward heard that an enemy was coming to the town, a man who had often attempted to ruin him and deliver him to his enemies, although lately they had been faithless (?). To find out the certainty of what he had heard he set out with only two men. When the man recognised Hereward on the road he immediately fled. Hereward directly followed on his track, from house to house, from garden to garden with his naked sword and a small shield in his hand, right into a great hall, where many local men were assembled at a love-feast. The man had nowhere to turn and Hereward being close upon him, he fled into the inner-part of the house and there put his head through an aperture and besought his pursuer to have mercy. Moved by generosity, as he was always most liberal in his doings, Hereward did not touch him nor did he inflict any damage in word or deed, but in the same way as he had come in he returned and passed out through the middle of the house. Not a man that was feasting, all being quite stupified, ventured even to grumble or to say anything opprobrious to him about the incident, as they had nothing to hand except drinking horns and wine-cups.

XXXI. How Hereward's wife assumed the habit of a nun at Crowland.

In the interval Hereward's wife, Turfrida, had begun to turn away from him, because he had at that time very often received messengers from a lady most powerful from her wealth (she was the wife of Earl Dolfinus), asking for licence from the King, which he could obtain for the mere asking as she had heard from the King's own mouth, if he were peaceably disposed and were willing to give him his adherance. For this purpose, and charmed with the beauty of the lady, Hereward gave his consent, because there was no one more beautiful or comely in the realm than she and hardly any one more eminent in wealth. Whereupon Hereward sent messengers to the King and demanded the lady aforesaid, declaring that he was willing to be reconciled with the King's Majesty. The King received the messengers graciously and appointed a day for him, agreeing to what he had demanded, adding that he had for a long time been wishing to receive him into his favour. But the real wife of Hereward, whom we have mentioned, by reason of this went to Crowland and chose the better life, taking the veil of a nun. On this account many evils happened to Hereward, because she was very wise and helpful in giving him advice when emergencies arose. Afterwards, as he himself often admitted, many things happened to him not so fortunately as in the time of his success.

XXXII. How Hereward overcame a certain very eminent Knight in single combat.

When Hereward was quietly walking at Brunneswald he met a certain Saxon soldier, a man of great courage and very tall, known as Letoltus. By means of his military skill and courage he was well known in many regions and much praised. Hereward, most courteous as he always was, first saluted him and asked him his name, dignity, and family. Not taking his words and questions in good part, Letoltus answered haughtily, calling Hereward a simpleton and a bore. So in the end in anger they came to blows. And not only these two, but their soldiers at the same time engaged; five accompanied the warrior and Hereward, three, namely Geri, Wenochus and Matelgar. As they fought, Geri soon laid low his opponent and attacked another of his mates. The other two soldiers soon overcame their adversaries. Meanwhile, Letoltus the eminent Knight did not cease fighting with Hereward, although his comrades were overcome, but Hereward did not allow his men to help him, saying then as always, when any man was fighting with him or with one of his men that it was an unworthy thing for two to fight against one, and that a man ought to fight with one man only or else surrender.

As the two men were long fighting, the result of the combat was still in doubt, contrary to all expectations, Hereward's sword broke off at the hilt and after turning round where the other was standing in astonishment, he fell down over his helmet. Immediately one of Hereward's soldiers, Geri addressed him, asking why he had forgotten what he had close by his side in such an emergency, and added that he wished he would yield to him the post against the foe; at which, greatly comforted, Hereward drew from its sheath another sword which he had forgotten and attacked the fellow more sharply, and at the very first blow, while he was supposed to be attacked on the head, he pierced the middle of the man's thigh bone. Yet for some time the warrior defended himself on his knees and declared that as long as life was in him he would never be willing to surrender or seem conquered. Seeing this,

Hereward greatly admiring him praised his valour and courage and ceased attacking him, leaving him and going on his road. And he said of the warrior to his men: "I have never found such a man, nor did I ever meet with his equal in courage, nor have I ever been in such peril when fighting against any man, nor have I ever had so much trouble in conquering a man."

XXXIII. How Hereward went to the King's court with his soldiers.

When Hereward was making his way to the King's court with the three men previously named, as he drew near he reflected it would not be a suitable way of meeting the King and straight away went back. On his return he led with him forty other distinguished soldiers, all of very great stature and efficient in warfare. They were remarkable if for nothing else for their mere appearance and equipment in arms. With his men Hereward was received by the King with ample kindness and honour, but he did not allow his company to remain among the royal courtiers and gave instructions for them to be entertained at the next town, lest by chance any disturbance should occur between them and his own men. Hereward with three soldiers only were received in the Palace, intending to treat with the King on the next day concerning his demands. On the following day the revered King himself went to see Hereward's soldiers and caused them, both with and without arms, to stand and march before him. And he was greatly delighted with them and praised them with compliments on their handsome appearance and height, and added that they were all bound to be very eminent in warfare. After this Hereward let them all go away to their own homes, except two soldiers and those with him. There he waited to receive in its entirety his father's land, after he had done homage to the King.

XXXIV. How Hereward fought with a soldier of the King's court and overcame him.

Now some of the King's soldiers at his court were indignant at what had taken place and felt aggrieved that foreigners and foes should have so suddenly come to such favour with the King's Majesty, and attempted to do Hereward some mischief; so they had a secret conversation with a very eminent soldier of their company, Ogger by name, and arranged that he should challenge Hereward to single combat, knowing that he could keep his hand from no man, if he were wantonly or haughtily provoked to a fight or contest of courage. For they thought that they would get some relief to their ill humour, even if he should refuse, as they were afraid in the King's presence to lift up a hand against him; but they very much hoped that he would be overcome by such a soldier, for he was taller than Hereward and to one merely looking at his eyes he gave the appearance of being much stronger. So they attempted to excite against him the aforesaid soldier, that he should wantonly challenge him to fight as though he had been insulted: but he was to do it secretly lest it should be disclosed to the King or his men before the combat took place. Hereward consented to him at last after having been repeatedly abused by the man. Immediately they went some distance to a grove, each accompanied by three companions, all bound by oath that no one of them should assist either, but only standing ready in case they should wish to come to an agreement or should rather choose to fight it out.

Thus the two engaged and fought for a long time. Often Hereward recommended him to desist from his enterprise, adding that it was a most stupid thing to go on fighting all day for nothing. But the soldier paid no attention to him, but deriving more confidence in himself as he supposed that Hereward often repeated his advice from fear or from exhaustion, or rather making sure that he already saw him defeated. More and more Ogger again and again Hereward began to give way in the hope of a peaceful settlement. But at last, Hereward, unable to bear it made a stand and as his custom both in war and in single contest was to fight manfully to the end, he stood up bravely against him, and did not desist until he had conquered him, his own right arm being severely wounded.

XXXV. How Hereward was accused by Robert de Horepol and put into prison.

Now these things had come to the knowledge of some of his enemies. Grudging his success they came to the court and brought to the King many false reports of Hereward, and they craftily impressed upon him that he should no longer have near him such men, traitors of his realm and enemies. That these people ought not to be admitted even to terms of agreement, but rather they should be handed over to punishment, or else be kept in perpetual imprisonment. The respected King listened lightly to these words, but in order to satisfy them he ordered Hereward at once to be taken into custody, and delivered to a certain worshipful man, Robert de Horepol, at Bedford. There Hereward remained for almost a year, merely bound with fetters. Unceasingly the Earl Warenne and Robert Malet and Ivo Taillebois opposed him and dissuaded the King from freeing him from custody, declaring that through Hereward's acts the country was not yet pacified. When Hereward's men heard of these things they dispersed, but often they sent a man in disguise to see him. He was Hereward's clerk, Leofric the Deacon by name who was very shrewd in all his doings, and even feigned folly in the place of a man of his learning, yet always acting wisely. On one occasion there went with Leofric, a man disguised as a cook seeking to purchase milk, a man of excessive caution among strangers full of humour. While they were present one day at the place of custody, the guardian of Hereward, namely Robert de Horepol, among other things commiserated with Hereward's plight, saying: "Alas! Alas! a man formerly famous for his bands of soldiers, and the leader and lord of so many very eminent men, is tomorrow to be taken hence, through the subtlety of Ivo Taillebois and delivered in the hands of a hateful man and sent to the castle at Buckingham. Oh! that those men whom formerly Hereward enriched with presents and raised with honours, would follow the traces of their master, coming against us on the march or in the Isle, and so set free their master and lord."

Hearing this these two men of Hereward, disclosed what they had heard to his soldiers and all his men, having received tokens from the imprisoned lord. They arranged to assemble at a certain place on the day when Hereward would pass in chains, for they had observed a wood through which the escort party would travel. On the arrival of the party with their prisoner, immediately Hereward's men rushed upon them unexpectedly overthrowing many before they could take up their light arms. Even so when others had armed themselves they put up a brave resistance, because they were so numerous - in fact all the soldiers from the castles around. To nearly all this superiority of numbers was the cause of death. When they could escape they refused to do so and at the end they were not even surrounded. Then among some who still survived, Hereward set free of ten chains, shouted out that the men of his respected gaoler must be carefully saved and that they must be allowed to leave unharmed, with Robert himself. Hereward, walked hither and thither among his men who were still fighting, telling them that Robert de Horepol had saved his life and at once they ceased pursuit. For as they came they marched last forming the rear and Hereward was led in front surrounded and chained. At last Robert de Horepol wished to depart with his comrades that had survived. Hereward returned him very many thanks, because he had kept him in custody courteously and had uniformly treated him with honour; and he asked Robert to intercede for him to the King.

XXXVI. How Robert de Horepol made a good report of Hereward to the King.

After this had taken place Robert de Horepol immediately went to the King's court telling him everything that had happened and how Hereward had been set free by his own men. Finally he delivered the message that Hereward should avail himself of the King's kindness and call to his mind how he had come to his court under the King's protection and safe conduct and that he had not rightly been put into prison and custody. But yet if the King would even now perform what he had then promised him, Hereward would serve his most dear lord in every way, since he knew that this wrong had not been done by him, but through the persuasion and craft of his enemies. After a little reflection upon these words the King replied that Hereward had not received right treatment; and when Robert saw that the King had taken his words in good part, he promptly related to him many things worth the telling about Hereward and his men, adding that for a little cause such a warrior ought not to be driven from him and his realm in whom there might be found great fidelity and trust. He further declared for certain that the King was rather inclined to rely on his old resources if a new disturbance arose in the land, unless in the King's eyes he could meet with favour rather than imprisonment and should receive from the King's goodness his father's land. Thereupon the King declared that Hereward ought by rights to have it, and gave command by his letters to Hereward and the men of his district that he ought to have the land of his father and to retain quiet possession of it; but that from henceforth he must be willing to cultivate peace, not folly, if he wished hereafter to retain the King's friendship.

Thus Hereward the famous warrior, in many places proved and well known, was received into favour by the King, and with his father's lands and possessions lived afterwards for many years, faithfully serving King William, and wholly devoted to his neighbours and friends. And so at last he rested in peace, and upon his soul may God have mercy. Amen.

END OF THE LIFE OF HEREWARD THE RENOWNED KNIGHT.

EAST END of Peterborough Cathedral. Beneath the Norman nave and choir can be seen the foundations of the Saxon monastery which was twice attacked by Hereward's army.

(Photo: T. Bevis)

GENEALOGICAL REFERENCE

THE WAKE FAMILY

THE BEST account of the Wake family down to about 1350 is in the Complete Peerage, New Edition, vol, XII, part 2 pages 259-304. This has numerous footnotes. There is an article by Dr. Edmund King in Northampton Past and Present, vol. V, No. 3, pages 167-173, 1975 called The Origins of the Wake Family - The Early History of the Barony of Bourne in Lincolnshire. The Architectural Society of the Diocese of Lincoln in their Report for 1861 printed a long article by the Rev. Edward Trollope called Hereward The Saxon Patriot; in the copy preserved at Delepre Abbey (Northamptonshire Records Office (JW Library 642) there is an heraldic pedigree appended. The Wake pedigree appears in Burke's Peerage for 1970, pages 2722-2727. An article by Sir Iain Moncrieffe of That Ilk, Ph.D., LL.B., F.S.A., Albany Herald, entitled Hereward and the Wakes, a genealogical survey, was reprinted in a booklet from The Genealogists' Magazine. The present holder of the baronetage is Sir Hereward Wake, M.C., D.L.

ADDENDUM

EVIDENCE THAT Hereward was married is attributed to a 12th Century MS "The Historia Croylandenis." The Cottonian Charter (xiii,9) compiled in 1407 for Edmund de Holand, Earl of Kent, giving his descent along the female line from Hereward, indicates that the Saxon patriot had a daughter named Turfrida after his mother. The genealogical descent from Richard de Rullos (c.1100), husband to Godiva, Hereward's grand-daughter, is irrefutable to the time of the Earl of Kent (1407). Richard, Duke of York, K.G., senior co-heir of the Wakes from 1425 placed the Wake torteaux on his white label over the Royal Arms.

WRITING IN about 1150, Geoffrey Gaimer, contrary to the final chapter of "De Gestis Herwardi" states that Hereward was treacherously slain by a Frenchman, Hugh D'Envermeu and Raul of Dol the Breton, who were being entertained by Hereward. Geoffrey Gaimer made a translation of "De Gestis Herwardi" under the title "Lestorie des Engles."

IT IS said that Hereward was buried at Crowland Abbey, a not ill-chosen place since, according to a chronicler, his first wife having taken the veil there in all probability would be interred at Crowland. On evidence of medieval manuscripts it seems that the tomb of Hereward and his wife, Turfrida, survived at Crowland in the 15th Century.

MUCH has been surmised as to Hereward's surname "Wake". Earliest surviving reference to the name appears in the Chronicon Petroburgense. Sir Iain Moncreiffe of That Ilk, Ph.D., LL.B., F.S.A. states in his article "Hereward and the Wakes" — "so far from casting doubt on the Wake connection with Hereward, it affords unsolicited corroboration of the then existence (many centuries ago) of the then general belief, anyway in the fen country around Peterborough, that their local hero (or rather, from the abbey point of view, bandit) Hereward was ancestor of the Wakes. The family had borne the surname of Wac or Wake for at least a generation before they married Baldwin Fitz Gilbert's co-heiress through whom descent from Hereward came".

THE controversial Causeway, be it at Stuntney or Aldreth, was undoubtedly very strongly garrisoned. William The Conqueror surrounded the Isle of Ely with a large army but the force of water surrounding it was more than adequate to keep the strongest army at bay. The insurgents built bulwarks on the island but there is no indication that the artificial mound "Cherry Hill", Ely, formed part of the defensive system at that time, or that any actual fighting took placed on the Isle after the Church had capitulated. It is a fact that the Fenland resisted the Norman intrusion most strongly and was the last to yield to the usurpation of the Norman invaders. It is said that Ely monks betrayed the Saxon resistance fighters but a strong desire of peace at least partly led to the monk's submission than the treachery that has been imputed to them.

Conflict on the Isle of Ely

THE ISLE OF ELY was a place of sanguinary conflict generally
spread over a period of five centuries. It formed an important
bastion and anyone holding it was a force to be reckoned with.
Danes attacked the Isle in the ninth century, and on one occasion
an armed force of Saxon inhabitants drove them off. The Danes
returned later and wreaked terrible vengeance on men and women,
pillaged the monasteries on the Fen islands and laid waste the
surrounding uplands.

The revolt of Hereward involves a core of truth in that it was
the final stand of almost-conquered Saxon England against the
might of the flying columns of William the Conqueror. In the wake
of previous rebellions against the King which he put down with
savage measure, a group of Saxons seized the Isle of Ely, and turned
it into a fortress. Then followed a period of lawlessness which
turned into guerrilla warfare. Upland villages were attacked by
the Isle insurgents, and the Norman army was positioned around the
fen perimeter to invest and blockade the islanders. Most of the
action occurred around the southern approaches to the Isle - in
the region of Soham and Alrehede - and continued for about a year.
The "war" came to an end not through military victory, but through
a treacherous act it is believed by Ely's abbot, under Norman
threat of the requisition of its estates elsewhere.

The Ely uprising was the most significant of a number of
rebellions which had taken place in the preceding four years.
It was thought not without good reason that at Ely on this natural
fastness, Saxons and their allies the Danes, could hold out
indefinitely against the King and eventually encourage such a surge
of patriotism for the Saxon cause that it would be impossible
for William the rule the land. An element in the affair which
ought not to be overlooked are the writings of a monk of Ely
(Liber Elien, pg. 223) inferring that the Ely revolt was wholly
justified, William of Normandy carrying out the most unheard of
cruelties whereby men were disinherited and reduced to poverty.
Many were forced to leave the land, their bodies mutilated. This
apparently was why noble Saxons such as Earl Morcar and Siward
Bearn, and Ethelwin, Bishop of Durham went to the Isle of Ely
(Anglo Saxon Chron. 1071). Furthermore, writes the monk, the
"minores populi" (peasants) were inhumanly treated by the King
and his followers. This applies to the ravages of the Norman
flying columns from vill to vill, devastating parts of Cambridge-

shire, after which vills in the region felt keen depreciation of
their former value.

The Norman invasion was particularly felt by the Cambridgeshire
peasantry and sokemen, generally classed as "free" and did, in fact,
thrive under the rule of King Harold. 1066 changed all that and
the free men living at "free, lordless villages" fell on evil days
between 1066 and 1086, the year of Domesday. From the number of
about 900, sokemen fell to 169 in that period. The dispossession
of the freemen's lands and the introduction of the new Norman land-
law put such pressure upon the peasantry and imposed a manorial
stamp upon it that was clearly intolerable. It was this state of
affairs that led to various revolts against King William.

Hereward's army it seems was made up of men who had suffered
in this process, and one can see the characteristics of a great,
final determination of the Saxon peasants and nobles to unite and
throw off the yoke of Norman persecution and implementation of
the horror of feudalism. Hereward, like Tochi of Weston Colville,
Wlwine of Swaffham, Turbern of Whaddon and Edwi of Eversden
(Domesday Book) belonged to a group of Saxon landowners who were
almost obliterated after the Normans' coming to England.

The Saxons enlisted the help of Danes in an attempt to diminish
the Norman threat and eventually drive the King's army into the sea.
In 1069 Sweyn had prepared an expedition to aggravate Saxons of
the east coast. Their longboats entered the Wash and infiltrated
Fenland rivers. "Then", says the Anglo-Saxon Chronicle, "the
Danish Bishop Christien, and Earl Osbern and their Danish retainers
came into Ely, and all the people of the Fens joined them, for they
believed that they should conquer the whole country". Just at that
time the abbacy of Peterborough on the edge of the Fens had fallen
vacant, and King William appointed a Norman abbot to supervise the
affairs of the monastery. On hearing of that appointment a number
of the Saxon tenants at Peterborough contacted the Danish fleet
and offered themselves as guides to the monastery. Numerous
treasures were seized and taken to Ely on its safe fastness.
The attack was recorded: " . . . early in the morning all the
outlaws came with many ships" (see the account by Hugo Candidus
in "Coenobii Burgensis Historia"). In June 1070 the Danes from
Ely attacked buildings around the monastery at Peterborough,
and burnt them but left the abbey intact. William the Conqueror
and Sweyn made peace and the Danes left Ely, but the Peterborough
tenants continued to resist the Normans.

Hereward was the man of the moment and at his feet was laid
hope for the Saxon race - the succeeding year formed the focal
point of this great resistance which resulted in great loss of life
among the Norman soldiery. Hereward went to Ely and made it a

rallying point. Many "took ship and went into the Isle intending to winter there" in safety, "beset by great meres and fens as though by a strong wall" (Florence of Worcester, Chronicon ex Chronicis). After several months King William, alarmed at this turn of events which was more of a threat to him than any other, appeared in person on the fen fringes "with ship-fyrd and land-fyrd (armies) (Liber Elien) and began setting up a blockade around the southern fens, to minimise the forays of the Isle-based rebels.

The prime places of hostility were the western and eastern sides of the island but there was military activity east of Ely. The Normans built a wooden fortress at Reach and were attacked at that point and also at Burwell. The insurgents could not be contained within the island fortress and small bands of armed men often sallied forth to aggravate the King's men at Reach and "set fire to the town of Burwell, inflicting mischief in every direction, and not only they, but also others running about" (De Gestis Herwardi. The siege was vexing to the King and at times he was depressed with the whole situation and withdrew to Brandon "giving up all hope of subduing the island" (Liber Elien). However, he "blocked up every outlet on the eastern shore by means of his boatmen" (Florence of Worcester). According to chroniclers many of the King's attempts to subdue the islanders ended in disaster and serious losses of men's lives.

It is probably inevitable that some myth crept into the accounts of the siege, yet it is abundantly clear that the Isle of Ely was the scene in c. 1071 of a great contest for the right to run the country. The event was recorded by several historians soon after the siege had ended, and their observation during the 12th and 13th centuries testify to that occasion which, in the writer's opinion is underrated in the annals of English military history. It was not just a hurried attempt to cast a thorn into the Conqueror's side, but began with the desire to defy the King and then to overthrow him and bring back the Saxon race to its rightful place in the land. Plans were made to this effect "the men of the Isle erecting outworks and bulwarks to oppose the enemy and make a vigorous resistance".

Legend greatly exaggerated the length of the siege. In certain accounts it is easy to believe that the resistance lasted almost seven years. That cannot be true, but more likely applies to the period of time that King William I met with minor and major uprisings throughout the length and breadth of the country. All of these were put down vigorously and cruelly. The Normans eventually gained the Isle not with force of arms, as in the previous rebellions elsewhere. Hereward and the core of his army, having been warned of the monk's betrayal melted away into the fen mists and into history. It appears that the campaign came

to an end inside a year. It was a disappointment to the Saxon
defenders when their allies, the Danes, departed. The Liber Elien
states that the monks of Ely, threatened with the loss of their
estates, negotiated with the King and "made arrangements for him
to come at once and secretly to the Isle, when Hereward and his
men were away foraging". At the end of 1071 William the Conqueror
stood victorious upon the Isle of Ely and by such victory, hollow
that it was, was truly the conqueror of the whole of the country.
"Hereward escaped through the fen with a few others" (Florence
of Worcester) and "all the outlaws surrendered" (Anglo Saxon
Chronicle). This applies to the peasants and others that had put
down the ploughshares and had taken up the sword and joined the
Saxon nobles on the Isle. Hereward and his skilled fighting men
seemed to have continued some kind of resistance against the
Normans, and in particular against the abbot of Peterborough, in
the safety of dense forests of Northamptonshire.

   With the siege of the Isle of Ely ended, the defeat of the
English in Eastern England was accomplished, and the Normans were
at last able to consolidate their gains. Forty Norman knights
that had crossed with the King from Normandy, were stationed at
Ely with as many monks and kept strict surveillance and occupied
the castle at Alrehede (Liber Elien). This was normal procedure
under Norman occupation whereby a conquering garrison sets down
roots in foreign soil, and the hierarchy of landholding society was
nurtured by the rule of military tenure. When the Domesday Book
had been completed in 1086 the Church recovered some of the lands
it had forfieted to military powers, and Ely, too, entered into a
period of reorganisation from which eventually the barony of Ely
was to emerge. (Peter of Blois; continuity of Ingulph's History of
Crowland).

*   *   *   *   *   *   *   *

THE CIVIL WARS

   It was not the last time that the Isle of Ely was subjected to
terror and siege. Feudal anarchy reached its peak in the reign of
Stephen (1135-1154), when in 1137 things had become so desperate
scribes wrote that "Christ and his saints slept" (Anglo-Saxon
Chronicle). This state of affairs was more acute in and around
the Cambridgeshire Fenland than anywhere else in the country.
The Isle of Ely afforded an ideal refuge to the rebellious barons
on at least two occasions - to Niel of Ely, Bishop of Ely in 1139
and in 1142 to Geoffrey de Mandeville. The former was forced to
surrender at Devizes castle, and came to Ely and raised the

42

standard of revolt. He prepared and re-fortified Alrehede castle
to resist attack (Cotton MS). As with Hereward, the bishop was
joined and provisioned by certain dignitaries of the area (Ibid.).
The King marched against the bishop and set about besieging the
Isle, viewing the matter as so serious that he, himself, marched
with his men (Ibid. Gesta Stephani). According to Anglia Sacra the
centre of the military focus was at Alrehede and a great many boats
gathered there and a bridge was built to carry soldiers across
the inhospitable water. The King encountered ponderous difficulties
and, similar to the Hereward account, entrance to the Isle was
gained through the treachery of an Ely monk who received as reward
the abbey of Ramsey (Ibid.). So fierce was the royal attack the
Isle defenders threw away their weapons and hid themselves in
remoter areas of the region. Bishop Niel and a few followers escaped
and were allowed safe custody by the Empress of Gloucester (Ibid.
63; Henry of Huntingdon, Historia Anglorum). Thus fell the Isle of
Ely to the King who exercised great control over it and great care
taken to secure the entrance at Alrehede.

As usual the Church at Ely suffered, being subjected to re-con-
fiscation. Niel was restored to the bishopric of Ely after the
Angevin victory at Lincoln in 1141, but when King Stephen's fortunes
had revived Bishop Niel was again exiled. In 1142 the Earl of Essex
(Geoffrey de Mandeville) and the Earl of Pembroke were ordered to
the Isle of Ely to disperse certain troublesome knights who had
assembled there. Geoffrey was met by fearful monks (Anglia Sacra)
and he threatened them with plunder and death. The possessions
of Ely were handed to the King. A few months elapsed and the King,
impressed by the Ely monks' pleas and the Pope's request, restored
Niel to the Isle of Ely and as a result the two Earls were obliged
to give up the Isle with its key into the Bishop's hand.

From 1142-43 there was peace within the Isle, but Bishop Niel
experienced a series of attacks at the Council of Northampton and
he went to Rome and appealed to the Pope in person (Ibid. 622).
It was during his absence that the Isle of Ely was taken over by
the King's former helper, Geoffrey de Mandeville, and he trans-
formed it into a seat of resistance against the ruler.
De Mandeville was an unpredictable man - with the King one moment
and against him the next. He was arrested at St. Albans at the end
of 1143 (De Antiquis Legibus Liber). King Stephen had every reason
to be highly suspicious of Bishop Niel and interpretted the
prelate's visit to Rome as an act of treason. Ely's monks had
invited Geoffrey De Mandeville to take over the Isle with its
fortifications.

43

He paid particilar attention to the strategic point at Alrehede
and also Fordham (Anglia Sacra) thus being able to communicate
with his allies in East Anglia (Gesta Stephani). Mandeville
strengthened his position in the Fens by establishing forces at
Ramsey and Benwick (Chron. Abb. Rames/Anglia Sacra). These
strongholds - both islands - gave him and his followers suitable
bases to launch attacks upon the uplands around and he laid the
whole countryside to waste. His extortionism grew worse and the
rebels extended their scenes of activity. Villages in the vicinity
were brutally attacked and yet another fortress was erected at
Wood Walton (Chron. Abb. Rames). Even the towns of Cambridge and
St. Ives were plundered and the countryside devastated. The
abbot of Ramsey who had been exiled put in a great amount of effort
to check the violence but to no avail.

Eventually the King arrived with a large force to press the
rebels hard and they took refuge in the marsh. While the King's
army gave attention to one part of the fen, Mandeville and his
men attacked another area. Finally the King established garrisons
of strategic value on the fen fringe - one at Burwell as directly
opposed to Mandeville's fortress at Fordham. Burwell castle was
never completed and in its incomplete state it was besieged by
Mandeville who could not tolerate it near his own garrison. The
castle at Burwell bode ill for him, as while he was busy with the
siege he carelessly removed his helmet and a keen-eyed archer
struck him down. Mandeville died a few days later at Mildenhall
(Chron. Abb. Rames). His son, Ernulf, continued his father's
work, but had little stomach to resist the King and was soon
obliged to give up Ramsey. A few months later the revolt had
completely ended. With peace restored to the Isle, Bishop Niel
returned and was reconciled with the King at Ipswich in 1144.
All the lands forfeited by the Church at Ely were recovered
and for the first time since Ely monastery became the seat of a
bishop he was able to administer the diocese without let or
hindrance.

Over many centuries the Isle of Ely enjoyed the reputation
as a place of refuge, though it harboured for most part,
undesireable rebels. Successive monarchs were aware of the Isle's
strategic importance. Henry III in a letter to the Archbishop of
Canterbury in 1256 aired his feelings on this matter of security
in the Fen region. He was justified in his thoughts, for Ely's
monks had elected their sub-prior to the bishopric before the
King's proctors had arrived. "Such an action," Henry wrote, "is not
only an infringement of the royal rights, it also imperils the
whole realm, for as history has proved, when the Dacians and

Saxons used to make war upon England, they found entry to the interior in the area around Ely." The King emphasised that it was of prime importance that whoever occupied the See of Ely should be a man of unswerving and trusted loyalty. (Close Rolls, 1256-9).

The King was undoubtedly inspired to broach this matter of loyalty bearing in mind the brief civil war that followed Magna Carta when a great measure of sympathy for the baronial cause was heard within the walls of the Major Church at Ely. It was not surprising therefore that once again rebels occupied the Isle of Ely. When King John's army marched by Bury St. Edmunds in about 1216 the baronial rebels there fled to the Isle and fortified the entrances and took up a defensive stance against an expected siege. But, for once the traditional and natural defences turned against the defenders. The marsh water froze over and two bands of royal troops crossed over the ice near Earith, overcame resistance and plundered the Isle and the great church.

In 1256 Henry III had such things on his mind and at the very outset of the constitutional struggle which beset him, it seemed that his fears were justified. Long before hostilities occurred in May 1260 the King ordered the Church at Ely to fortify the entrances of the Isle and guard them from sunset to sunrise, so that no unlawful person could enter, and thus avert possible disaster to the realm. Even so, in 1266 after the resistance at Kenilworth a section of the rebels marched through Cambridgeshire and occupied the Isle of Ely, despite the pledge by the Bishop to keep the Isle for the King. From this base they pillaged the surrounding countryside.

The rebels were most notorious and chronicles made emphatic reference at them. Without regard of person or place, the rebels from the Isle took rich persons and held them for ransom, and carried off to Ely whatever they could lay hands on, corn and malt, oxen and sheep (Liber de Bernewelle). They eneterd Cambridge and compelled burgesses to pay fines of 300 marks or see their town burn to ashes. The rebels even reached Norwich and plundered it a whole night and morning (Historia Anglicana). At Bury St. Edmunds "some ruffians . . . from the Isle of Ely, siezed the horses . . . concealed in the inner court of the abbey, and leading them through the infirmary, carried them off to the Isle of Ely. A monk of the house having pursued them, made a clear statement of the facts to the Isle authorities. At last the islanders, actually the rebels, accepted his statement and committed the ruffians . . . with theirhorses to the judgement of the monk. When they brought back the horses most devoutly to the altar of St. Edmund, they laid their swords which they had irreverently drawn against the liberty of St. Edmund, upon the shrine of the saint in token of their presumption." (Mem. of St. Edmund's).

Thus is briefly written a passage in the chequered history from the years of Danish incursion against the monastery and villages of the Isle of Ely which were burned to the ground and inhabitants put to the sword and axe, to the months of the epic struggle of Hereward against the Norman invader. The civil wars of the 13th century with their repeated sanguinary conclusions did not bring an end to military intrigue within the Isle. Another son of the Fens - Oliver Cromwell - gathered a host of "God-fearing, honest men" from the flatlands and drilled them into a new, invincible army known throughout Europe for skill and tenacity, marching to great victories, hands on swords and bibles. In our own time the Isle of Ely sent hundreds of young men to Singapore, untrained for jungle warfare, let down by their generals, and committed to years of captivity in the green hell of the Far East. The majority did not return.